An Account of the Foxglove and some of its Medical Uses With Practical Remarks on Dropsy and Other Diseases

William Withering

Alpha Editions

This Edition Published in 2021

ISBN: 9789354591471

Design and Setting By
Alpha Editions
www.alphaedis.com
Email – info@alphaedis.com

As per information held with us this book is in Public Domain.
This book is a reproduction of an important historical work. Alpha Editions uses the best technology to reproduce historical work in the same manner it was first published to preserve its original nature. Any marks or number seen are left intentionally to preserve its true form.

TABLE OF CONTENTS

PREFACE — - 1 -

INTRODUCTION — - 4 -

OF THE PLATE — - 11 -

EXPLANATION — - 12 -

FOOTNOTES: — - 12 -

AN ACCOUNT OF THE INTRODUCTION OF FOXGLOVE INTO MODERN PRACTICE — - 13 -

CASES, IN WHICH THE DIGITALIS WAS GIVEN BY THE DIRECTION OF THE AUTHOR — - 19 -

1775. — - 19 -

CASE I. — - 19 -

1776. CASE II. — - 19 -

CASE III. — - 19 -

CASE IV. — - 20 -

CASE V. — - 22 -

1777. — - 23 -

CASE VI. — - 23 -

CASE VII. — - 23 -

CASE VIII. — - 24 -

CASE IX. — - 24 -

CASE X.	- 24 -
CASE XI.	- 25 -
CASE XII.	- 25 -
CASE XIII.	- 26 -
1778. CASE XIV.	- 26 -
CASE XV.	- 26 -
CASE XVI.	- 26 -
CASE XVII.	- 26 -
CASE XVIII.	- 27 -
CASE XIX.	- 28 -
1779.	- 28 -
CASE XX.	- 28 -
CASE XXI.	- 29 -
CASE XXII.	- 29 -
CASE XXIII.	- 30 -
CASE XXIV.	- 30 -
CASE XXV.	- 31 -
CASE XXVI.	- 31 -
CASE XXVII.	- 31 -
1780. CASE XXVIII.	- 33 -

CASE XXIX.	- 34 -
CASE XXX.	- 34 -
CASE XXXI.	- 34 -
CASE XXXII.	- 35 -
CASE XXXIII.	- 35 -
CASE XXXIV.	- 35 -
CASE XXXV.	- 36 -
CASE XXXVI.	- 36 -
CASE XXXVII.	- 36 -
CASE XXXVIII.	- 36 -
CASE XXXIX.	- 37 -
CASE XL.	- 37 -
CASE XLI.	- 37 -
CASE XLII.	- 37 -
CASE XLIII.	- 37 -
INTERVALS.	- 40 -
CASE XLIV.	- 40 -
CASE XLV.	- 40 -
CASE XLVI.	- 40 -
CASE XLVII.	- 41 -
CASE XLVIII.	- 41 -

CASE XLIX.	- 41 -
CASE L.	- 41 -
CASE LI.	- 42 -
CASE LII.	- 42 -
CASE LIII.	- 43 -
CASE LIV.	- 43 -
CASE LV.	- 44 -
CASE LVI.	- 44 -
CASE LVII.	- 45 -
1781. CASE LVIII.	- 45 -
CASE LIX.	- 45 -
CASE LX.	- 46 -
CASE LXI.	- 46 -
CASE LXII.	- 46 -
CASE LXIII.	- 47 -
CASE LXIV.	- 47 -
CASE LXV.	- 47 -
CASE LXVI.	- 47 -
CASE LXVII.	- 48 -
CASE LXVIII.	- 48 -
CASE LXIX.	- 48 -

CASE LXX.	- 49 -
CASE LXXI.	- 49 -
CASE LXXII.	- 49 -
CASE LXXIII.	- 49 -
CASE LXXIV.	- 49 -
CASE LXXV.	- 50 -
CASE LXXVI.	- 50 -
CASE LXXVII.	- 50 -
CASE LXXVIII.	- 51 -
CASE LXXIX.	- 51 -
CASE LXXX.	- 51 -
CASE LXXXI.	- 51 -
CASE LXXXII.	- 52 -
1782. CASE LXXXIII.	- 52 -
CASE LXXXIV.	- 52 -
CASE LXXXV.	- 52 -
CASE LXXXVI.	- 53 -
CASE LXXXVII.	- 53 -
CASE LXXXVIII.	- 53 -
CASE LXXXIX.	- 54 -
CASE XC.	- 54 -

CASE XCI.	- 54 -
CASE XCII.	- 54 -
CASE XCIII.	- 54 -
CASE XCIV.	- 55 -
CASE XCV.	- 55 -
CASE XCVI.	- 55 -
CASE XCVII.	- 55 -
CASE XCVIII.	- 56 -
CASE XCIX.	- 56 -
CASE C.	- 56 -
CASE CI.	- 57 -
CASE CII.	- 57 -
CASE CIII.	- 57 -
CASE CIV.	- 57 -
CASE CV.	- 58 -
CASE CVI.	- 58 -
CASE CVII.	- 58 -
1783.	- 59 -
CASE CVIII.	- 59 -
CASE CIX.	- 59 -
CASE CX.	- 59 -

CASE CXI.	- 60 -
CASE CXII.	- 60 -
CASE CXIII.	- 60 -
CASE CXIV.	- 60 -
CASE CXV.	- 60 -
CASE CXVI.	- 60 -
CASE CXVII.	- 61 -
CASE CXVIII.	- 61 -
CASE CXIX.	- 62 -
CASE CXX.	- 62 -
CASE CXXI.	- 63 -
CASE CXXII.	- 63 -
1784. CASE CXXIII.	- 64 -
CASE CXXIV.	- 64 -
CASE CXXV.	- 64 -
CASE CXXVI.	- 65 -
CASE CXXVII.	- 65 -
CASE CXXVIII.	- 66 -
CASE CXXIX.	- 66 -
CASE CXXX.	- 66 -
CASE CXXXI.	- 67 -

CASE CXXXII.	- 67 -
CASE CXXXIII.	- 68 -
CASE CXXXIV.	- 68 -
CASE CXXXV.	- 68 -
CASE CXXXVI.	- 68 -
CASE CXXXVII.	- 69 -
CASE CXXXVIII.	- 69 -
CASE CXXXIX.	- 70 -
CASE CXL.	- 70 -
CASE CXLI.	- 70 -
CASE CXLII.	- 71 -
CASE CXLIII.	- 71 -
CASE CXLIV.	- 71 -
CASE CXLV.	- 72 -
CASE CXLVI.	- 72 -
CASE CXLVII.	- 72 -
CASE CXLVIII.	- 73 -
CASE CXLIX.	- 73 -
CASE CL.	- 73 -
CASE CLI.	- 73 -
CASE CLII.	- 74 -

CASE CLIII.	- 74 -
CASE CLIV.	- 74 -
CASE CLV.	- 75 -
CASE CLVI.	- 75 -
1785.	- 75 -
FOOTNOTES:	- 75 -
HOSPITAL CASES, UNDER THE DIRECTION OF THE AUTHOR	- 76 -
CASE CLVII.	- 76 -
CASE CLVIII.	- 76 -
CASE CLIX.	- 76 -
CASE CLX.	- 77 -
CASE CLXI.	- 78 -
CASE CLXII.	- 78 -
CASE CLXIII.	- 80 -
COMMUNICATIONS FROM CORRESPONDENTS	- 81 -
CASE.	- 85 -
CASE I.	- 89 -
CASE II.	- 89 -
CASE I.	- 90 -
CASE II.	- 91 -

CASE III.	- 91 -
CASE IV.	- 91 -
CASE V.	- 91 -
CASE VI.	- 92 -
CASE VII.	- 92 -
CASE VIII.	- 92 -
CASE IX.	- 92 -
CASE X.	- 92 -
CASE XI.	- 92 -
CASE XII.	- 92 -
CASE XIII.	- 93 -
CASE XIV.	- 93 -
CASE XV.	- 93 -
CASE XVI.	- 94 -
CASE XVII.	- 94 -
CASE XVIII.	- 94 -
CASE XIX.	- 94 -
CASE XX.	- 94 -
CASE XXI.	- 94 -
CASE XXII.	- 95 -
CASE XXIII.	- 95 -

CASE XXIV.	- 95 -
REMARKS.	- 95 -
REMARKS.	- 98 -
CASE II.	- 100 -
CASE I.	- 102 -
CASE II.	- 103 -
CASE III.	- 104 -
CASE I.	- 106 -
CASE II.	- 106 -
CASE III.	- 107 -
CASE I.	- 109 -
CASE II.	- 110 -
CASE I.	- 115 -
CASE II.	- 117 -
CASE III.	- 119 -
CASE IV.	- 120 -
CASE V.	- 120 -
CASE VI.	- 121 -
CASE VII.	- 121 -
CASE VIII.	- 122 -
FOOTNOTES:	- 122 -

OF THE PREPARATIONS AND DOSES, OF THE FOXGLOVE	- 124 -
EFFECTS, RULES, AND CAUTIONS	- 127 -
FOOTNOTES:	- 129 -
CONSTITUTION OF PATIENTS	- 130 -
INFERENCES.	- 131 -
PRACTICAL REMARKS ON DROPSY, AND SOME OTHER DISEASES	- 133 -
ANASARCA.	- 133 -
ASCITES.	- 134 -
ASCITES AND ANASARCA.	- 134 -
ASCITES, ANASARCA, AND HYDROTHORAX.	- 134 -
ASTHMA.	- 134 -
ASTHMA AND ANASARCA.	- 134 -
ASTHMA AND ASCITES.	- 135 -
ASTHMA, ASCITES, AND ANASARCA.	- 135 -
EPILEPSY.	- 135 -
HYDATID DROPSY.	- 135 -
HYDROCEPHALUS.	- 135 -
HYDROTHORAX.	- 137 -
HYDROTHORAX AND ANASARCA.	- 138 -
INSANITY.	- 138 -

NEPHRITIS CALCULOSA.	- 138 -
OVARIUM DROPSY.	- 138 -
OVARIUM DROPSY WITH ANASARCA.	- 139 -
PHTHISIS PULMONALIS.	- 139 -
PUERPERAL ANASARCA.	- 141 -
FOOTNOTES:	- 141 -

PREFACE

After being frequently urged to write upon this subject, and as often declining to do it, from apprehension of my own inability, I am at length compelled to take up the pen, however unqualified I may still feel myself for the task.

The use of the Foxglove is getting abroad, and it is better the world should derive some instruction, however imperfect, from my experience, than that the lives of men should be hazarded by its unguarded exhibition, or that a medicine of so much efficacy should be condemned and rejected as dangerous and unmanageable.

It is now about ten years since I first began to use this medicine. Experience and cautious attention gradually taught me how to use it. For the last two years I have not had occasion to alter the modes of management; but I am still far from thinking them perfect.

It would have been an easy task to have given select cases, whose successful treatment would have spoken strongly in favour of the medicine, and perhaps been flattering to my own reputation. But Truth and Science would condemn the procedure. I have therefore mentioned every case in which I have prescribed the Foxglove, proper or improper, successful or otherwise. Such a conduct will lay me open to the censure of those who are disposed to censure, but it will meet the approbation of others, who are the best qualified to be judges.

To the Surgeons and Apothecaries, with whom I am connected in practice, both in this town and at a distance, I beg leave to make this public acknowledgment, for the assistance they so readily afforded me, in perfecting some of the cases, and in communicating the events of others.

The ages of the patients are not always exact, nor would the labour of making them so have been repaid by any useful consequences. In a few instances accuracy in that respect was necessary, and there it has been attempted; but in general, an approximation towards the truth, was supposed to be sufficient.

The cases related from my own experience, are generally written in the shortest form I could contrive, in order to save time and labour. Some of them are given more in detail, when particular circumstances made such detail necessary; but the cases communicated by other practitioners, are given in their own words.

I must caution the reader, who is not a practitioner in physic, that no general deductions, decisive upon the failure or success of the medicine, can be drawn from the cases I now present to him. These cases must be considered as the most hopeless and deplorable that exist; for physicians are seldom consulted in chronic diseases, till the usual remedies have failed: and, indeed, for some years, whilst I was less expert in the management of the Digitalis, I seldom prescribed it, but when the failure of every other method compelled me to do it; so that upon the whole, the instances I am going to adduce, may truly be considered as cases lost to the common run of practice, and only snatched from destruction, by the efficacy of the Digitalis; and this in so remarkable a manner, that, if the properties of that plant had not been discovered, by far the greatest part of these patients must have died.

There are men who will hardly admit of any thing which an author advances in support of a favorite medicine, and I allow they may have some cause for their hesitation; nor do I expect they will wave their usual modes of judging upon the present occasion. I could wish therefore that such readers would pass over what I have said, and attend only to the communications from correspondents, because they cannot be supposed to possess any unjust predilection in favour of the medicine: but I cannot advise them to this step, for I am certain they would then close the book, with much higher notions of the efficacy of the plant than what they would have learnt from me. Not that I want faith in the discernment or in the veracity of my correspondents, for they are men of established reputation; but the cases they have sent me are, with some exceptions, too much selected. They are not upon this account less valuable in themselves, but they are not the proper premises from which to draw permanent conclusions.

I wish the reader to keep in view, that it is not my intention merely to introduce a new diuretic to his acquaintance, but one which, though not infallible, I believe to be much more certain than any other in present use.

After all, in spite of opinion, prejudice, or error, Time will fix the real value upon this discovery, and determine whether I have imposed upon myself and others, or contributed to the benefit of science and mankind.

Birmingham, 1st July, 1785.

INTRODUCTION

The Foxglove is a plant sufficiently common in this island, and as we have but one species, and that so generally known, I should have thought it superfluous either to figure or describe it; had I not more than once seen the leaves of Mullein gathered for those of Foxglove. On the continent of Europe too, other species are found, and I have been informed that our species is very rare in some parts of Germany, existing only by means of cultivation, in gardens.

Our plant is the Digitalis purpurea of Linnæus. It belongs to the 2d order of the 14th class, or the Didynamia Angiospermia. The essential characters of the genus are, Cup with 5 divisions. Blossom bell-shaped, bulging. Capsule egg-shaped, 2-celled.—Linn.

DIGITA'LIS purpu'rea. Little leaves of the empalement egg-shaped, sharp. Blossoms blunt; the upper lip entire. Linn.

References to Figures. These are disposed in the order of comparative excellence.

- Rivini monopet. 104.
- Flora danica, 74, parts of fructification.
- Tournefort Institutiones. 73, A, E, L, M.
- Fuchsii Hist. Plant. 893, copied in
- Tragi stirp. histor. 889.
- J. Bauhini histor. Vol. ii. 812. 3, and
- Lonicera 74, 1.
- Blackwell. auct. 16.
- Dodonœi pempt. stirp. hist. 169, reprinted in
- Gerard emacul. 790, 1, and copied in
- Parkinson Theatr. botanic. 653, 1.
- Gerard, first edition, 646, 1.
- Histor. Oxon. Morison. V. 8, row 1. 1.

- Flor. danic. 74, the reduced figure.

Blossom. The bellying part on the inside sprinkled with spots like little eyes. Leaves wrinkled. Linn.

Blossom. Rather tubular than bell-shaped, bulging on the under side, purple; the narrow tubular part at the base, white. Upper lip sometimes slightly cloven.

Chives. Threads crooked, white. Tips yellow.

Pointal. Seed-bud greenish. Honey-cup at its base more yellow. Summit cloven.

S. Vess. Capsule not quite so long as the cup.

Root. Knotty and fibrous.

Stem. About 4 feet high; obscurely angular; leafy.

Leaves. Slightly but irregularly serrated, wrinkled; dark green above, paler underneath. Lower leaves egg-shaped; upper leaves spear-shaped. Leaf-stalks fleshy; bordered.

Flowers. Numerous, mostly growing from one side of the stem and hanging down one over another. Floral-leaves sitting, taper-pointed. The numerous purple blossoms hanging down, mottled within; as wide and nearly half as long as the finger of a common-sized glove, are sufficient marks whereby the most ignorant may distinguish this from every other British plant; and the leaves ought not to be gathered for use but when the plant is in blossom.

Place. Dry, gravelly or sandy soils; particularly on sloping ground. It is a biennial, and flowers from the middle of June to the end of July.

I have not observed that any of our cattle eat it. The root, the stem, the leaves, and the flowers have a bitter herbaceous taste, but I don't perceive that nauseous bitter which has been attributed to it.

This plant ranks amongst the LURIDÆ, one of the Linnæan orders in a natural system. It has for congenera, Nicotiana, Atropa, Hyoscyamus, Datura, Solanum, &c. so that from the knowledge we possess of the virtues of those plants, and reasoning from botanical analogy, we might be led to guess at something of its properties.

I intended in this place to have traced the history of its effects in diseases from the time of Fuchsius, who first describes it, but I have been anticipated in this intention by my very valuable friend, Dr. Stokes of Stourbridge, who has lately sent me the following

Historical View of the Properties of Digitalis.

Fuchsius in his hist. stirp. 1542, is the first author who notices it. From him it receives its name of Digitalis, in allusion to the German name of Fingerhut, which signifies a finger-stall, from the blossoms resembling the finger of a glove.

Sensible Qualities. Leaves bitterish, very nauseous. Lewis Mat. med. i. 342.

Sensible Effects. Some persons, soon after eating of a kind of omalade, into which the leaves of this, with those of several other plants, had entered as an ingredient, found themselves much indisposed, and were presently after attacked with vomitings. Dodonæus pempt. 170.

It is a medicine which is proper only for strong constitutions, as it purges very violently, and excites excessive vomitings. Ray. hist. 767.

Boerhaave judges it to be of a poisonous nature, hist. plant. but Dr. Alston ranks it among those indigenous vegetables, "which, though now disregarded, are medicines of great virtue, and scarcely inferior to any that the Indies afford." Lewis Mat. med. i. p. 343.

Six or seven spoonfuls of the decoction produce nausea and vomiting, and purge; not without some marks of a deleterious quality. Haller hist. n. 330 from Aerial Infl. p. 49, 50.

The following is an abridged Account of its Effects upon Turkeys.

M. Salerne, a physician at Orleans, having heard that several turkey pouts had been killed by being fed with Foxglove leaves, instead of mullein, he gave some of the same leaves to a large vigorous turkey. The bird was so much affected that he could not stand upon his legs, he appeared drunk, and his excrements became reddish. Good nourishment restored him to health in eight days.

Being then determined to push the experiment further, he chopped some more leaves, mixed them with bran, and gave them to a vigorous turkey cock which weighed seven pounds. This bird soon appeared drooping and melancholy; his feathers stared, his neck became pale and retracted. The leaves were given him for four days, during which time he took about half a handful. These leaves had been gathered about eight days, and the winter was far advanced. The excrements, which are naturally green and well formed, became, from the first, liquid and reddish, like those of a dysenteric patient.

The animal refusing to eat any more of this mixture which had done him so much mischief, I was obliged to feed him with bran and water only; but notwithstanding this, he continued drooping, and without appetite. At times he was seized with convulsions, so strong as to throw him down; in the intervals he walked as if drunk; he did not attempt to perch, he uttered plaintive cries. At length he refused all nourishment. On the fifth or sixth day the excrements became as white as chalk; afterwards yellow, greenish, and black. On the eighteenth day he died, greatly reduced in flesh, for he now weighed only three pounds.

On opening him we found the heart, the lungs, the liver, and gall-bladder shrunk and dried up; the stomach was quite empty, but not deprived of its villous coat. Hist. de l'Academ. 1748. p. 84.

Epilepsy.—"It hath beene of later experience found also to be effectual against the falling sicknesse, that divers have been cured thereby; for after the taking of the Decoct. manipulor. ii. c. polypod. quercin. contus. ʒiv. in cerevisia, they that have been troubled with it twenty-six years, and have fallen once in a weeke, or two or three times in a moneth, have not fallen once in fourteen or fifteen moneths, that is until the writing hereof."

Parkinson, p. 654.

Scrophula.—"The herb bruised, or the juice made up into an ointment, and applied to the place, hath been found by late experience to be availeable for the King's Evill." Park. p. 654.

Several hereditary instances of this disease said to have been cured by it. Aereal Influences, p. 49, 50, quoted by Haller, hist. n. 330.

A man with scrophulous ulcers in various parts of the body, and which in the right leg were so virulent that its amputation was proposed, cured by succ. express. cochl. i. bis intra xiv. dies, in ½ pintæ cerevisiæ calidæ.

The leaves remaining after the pressing out of the juice, were applied every day to the ulcers. Pract. ess. p. 40. quoted by Murray apparat. medicam. i. p. 491.

A young woman with a scrophulous tumour of the eye, a remarkable swelling of the upper lip, and painful tumours of the joints of the fingers, much relieved; but the medicine was left off, on account of its violent effects on the constitution. Ib. p. 42 quoted as above.

A man with scrophulous tumour of the right elbow, attended for three years with excruciating pains, was nearly cured by four doses of the juice taken once a month. Ib. p. 43. as above.

The physicians and surgeons of the Worcester Infirmary have employed it in ointments and poultices with remarkable efficacy. Ib. p. 44. It was recommended to them by Dr. Baylies of Evesham, now of Berlin, as a remedy for this disease. Dr. Wall gave it a tryal, as well externally as internally, but their experiments did not lead them to observe any other properties in it, than those of a highly nauseating medicine and drastic purgative.

Wounds. In considerable estimation for the healing all kinds of wounds, Lobel. adv. 245.

Principally of use in ulcers, which discharge considerably, being of little advantage in such as are dry. Hulse, in R. hist. 768.

Doctor Baylies, physician to his Prussian Majesty, informed me, when at Berlin, that he employed it with great success in caries, and obstinate sore legs.

Dyspnœa Pituitosa Sauvages i. 657.—"Boiled in water, or wine, and drunken doth cut and consume the thicke toughnesse of grosse, and slimie flegme, and naughtie humours. The same, or boiled with honied water or sugar, doth scoure and clense the brest, ripeneth and bringeth foorth tough and clammie flegme. It openeth also the stoppage of the liver spleene and milt, and of the inwarde parts." Gerarde hist. ed. I p. 647.

"Whensoever there is need of a rarefying or extenuating of tough flegme or viscous humours troubling the chest,—the decoction or juice hereof made up with sugar or honey is availeable, as also to clense and purge the body both upwards and downwards sometimes, of tough flegme, and clammy humours, notwithstanding that these qualities are found to bee in it, there are but few physitions in our times that put it to these uses, but it is in a manner wholly neglected."

Parkinson, p. 654.

Previous to the year 1777, you informed me of the great success you had met with in curing dropsies by means of the fol. Digitalis, which you then considered as a more certain diuretic than any you had ever tried. Some time afterwards, Mr. Russel, surgeon, of Worcester, having heard of the success which had attended some cases in which you had given it, requested me to obtain for him any information you might be inclined to communicate respecting its use. In consequence of this application, you wrote to me in the following terms.

In a letter which I received from you in London, dated September 29, 1778, you write as follows:—"I wish it was as easy to write upon the Digitalis—I despair of pleasing myself or instructing others, in a subject so difficult. It is much easier to write upon a disease than upon a remedy. The former is in the hands of nature, and a faithful observer, with an eye of tolerable judgment, cannot fail to delineate a likeness. The latter will ever be subject to the whims, the inaccuracies, and the blunders of mankind."—

In my notes I find the following memorandum—"February 20th, 1779, gave an account of Doctor Withering's practice, with the precautions necessary to its success, to the Medical Society at Edinburgh."—In the course of that year, the Digitalis was prescribed in the Edinburgh Infirmary, by Dr. Hope, and in the following year, whilst I was Clerk to Dr. Home, as Clinical Professor, I had a favourable opportunity of observing its sensible effects.

In one case in which it was given properly at first, the urine began to flow freely on the second day. On the third, the swellings began to subside. The dose was then increased more than quadruple in the twenty-four hours. On the fifth day sickness came on, and much purging, but the urine still increased though the pulse sunk to 50. On the 7th day, a quadruple dose of the infusion was ordered to be taken every third hour, so as to bring on nausea again. The pulse fell to forty-four, and at length to thirty-five in a minute. The patient gradually sunk and died on the sixteenth day; but previous to her death, for two or three days, her pulse rose to near one hundred.—It is needless to observe to you, how widely the treatment of this case differed from the method which you have found so successful.

OF THE PLATE

The figure of the Foxglove, facing the Title Page, is copied by the permission and under the inspection of Mr. Curtis, from his admirable work, entitled Flora Londinensis. The accuracy of the drawings, the beauty of the colouring, the full descriptions, the accurate specific distinctions, and the uses of the different plants, cannot fail to recommend that work to the patronage of all who are interested in the encouragement of genius, or the promotion of useful knowledge.

EXPLANATION

Fig. 1. The Empalement.

Fig. 2, 3, 4. Four Chives two long and two short. Tips at first large, turgid, oval, touching at bottom, of a yellowish colour, and often spotted; lastly changing both their form and situation in a singular manner.

Fig. 5, 6, 7. Seed-bud rather conical, of a yellow green colour. Shaft simple. Summit cloven.

Fig. 8. Honey-cup a gland, surrounding the bottom of the Seed-bud.

Fig. 9. Seed-vessel, a pointed oval Capsule, of two cells and two valves, the lowermost valve splitting in two.

Fig. 10. Seeds numerous, blackish, small, lopped at each end.

FOOTNOTES:

Verbascum of Linnæus.

The trivial name purpurea is not a very happy one, for the blossoms though generally purple, are sometimes of a pure white.

See the extract from this letter at page 5.

AN ACCOUNT OF THE INTRODUCTION of FOXGLOVE INTO MODERN PRACTICE

As the more obvious and sensible properties of plants, such as colour, taste, and smell, have but little connexion with the diseases they are adapted to cure; so their peculiar qualities have no certain dependence upon their external configuration. Their chemical examination by fire, after an immense waste of time and labour, having been found useless, is now abandoned by general consent. Possibly other modes of analysis will be found out, which may turn to better account; but we have hitherto made only a very small progress in the chemistry of animal and vegetable substances. Their virtues must therefore be learnt, either from observing their effects upon insects and quadrupeds; from analogy, deduced from the already known powers of some of their congenera, or from the empirical usages and experience of the populace.

The first method has not yet been much attended to; and the second can only be perfected in proportion as we approach towards the discovery of a truly natural system; but the last, as far as it extends, lies within the reach of every one who is open to information, regardless of the source from whence it springs.

It was a circumstance of this kind which first fixed my attention on the Foxglove.

In the year 1775, my opinion was asked concerning a family receipt for the cure of the dropsy. I was told that it had long been kept a secret by an old woman in Shropshire, who had sometimes made cures after the more regular practitioners had failed. I was informed also, that the effects produced were violent vomiting and purging; for the diuretic effects seemed to have been overlooked. This medicine was composed of twenty or more different herbs; but it was not very difficult for one conversant in these subjects, to perceive, that the active herb could be no other than the Foxglove.

My worthy predecessor in this place, the very humane and ingenious Dr. Small, had made it a practice to give his advice to the poor during one hour in a day. This practice, which I continued until we had an Hospital opened for the reception of the sick poor, gave me an opportunity of putting my ideas into execution in a variety of cases; for the number of poor who thus applied for advice, amounted to between two and three thousand annually. I soon found the Foxglove to be a very powerful diuretic; but then, and for a considerable time afterwards, I gave it in doses very much too large, and urged its continuance too long; for misled by reasoning from the effects of the squill, which generally acts best upon the kidneys when it excites nausea, I wished to produce the same effect by the Foxglove. In this mode of prescribing, when I had so many patients to attend to in the space of one, or at most of two hours, it will not be expected that I could be very particular, much less could I take notes of all the cases which occurred. Two or three of them only, in which the medicine succeeded, I find mentioned amongst my papers. It was from this kind of experience that I ventured to assert, in the Botanical Arrangement published in the course of the following spring, that the Digitalis purpurea "merited more attention than modern practice bestowed upon it."

I had not, however, yet introduced it into the more regular mode of prescription; but a circumstance happened which accelerated that event. My truly valuable and respectable friend, Dr. Ash, informed me that Dr. Cawley, then principal of Brazen Nose College, Oxford, had been cured of a Hydrops Pectoris, by an empirical exhibition of the root of the Foxglove, after some of the first physicians of the age had declared they could do no more for him. I was now determined to pursue my former ideas more vigorously than before, but was too well aware of the uncertainty which must attend on the exhibition of the root of a biennial plant, and therefore continued to use the leaves. These I had found to vary much as to dose, at different seasons of the year; but I expected, if gathered always in one condition of the plant, viz. when it was in its flowering state, and carefully dried, that the dose might be ascertained as exactly as that of any other medicine; nor have I been disappointed in this expectation. The more I saw of the great powers of this plant, the more it seemed necessary to bring the doses of it to the greatest possible accuracy. I suspected that this degree of accuracy was not reconcileable with the use of a decoction, as it depended not only upon the care of those who had the preparation of it, but it was easy to conceive from the analogy of another plant of the same natural order, the tobacco, that its active properties might be impaired by long boiling. The decoction was therefore discarded, and the infusion substituted in its place. After this I began to use the leaves in powder, but I still very often prescribe the infusion.

Further experience convinced me, that the diuretic effects of this medicine do not at all depend upon its exciting a nausea or vomiting; but, on the contrary, that though the increased secretion of urine will frequently succeed to, or exist along with these circumstances, yet they are so far from being friendly or necessary, that I have often known the discharge of urine checked, when the doses have been imprudently urged so as to occasion sickness.

If the medicine purges, it is almost certain to fail in its desired effect; but this having been the case, I have seen it afterwards succeed when joined with small doses of opium, so as to restrain its action on the bowels.

In the summer of the year 1776, I ordered a quantity of the leaves to be dried, and as it then became possible to ascertain its doses, it was gradually adopted by the medical practitioners in the circle of my acquaintance.

In the month of November 1777, in consequence of an application from that very celebrated surgeon, Mr. Russel, of Worcester, I sent him the following account, which I choose to introduce here, as shewing the ideas I then entertained of the medicine, and how much I was mistaken as to its real dose.—"I generally order it in decoction. Three drams of the dried leaves, collected at the time of the blossoms expanding, boiled in twelve to eight ounces of water. Two spoonfuls of this medicine, given every two hours, will sooner or later excite a nausea. I have sometimes used the green leaves gathered in winter, but then I order three times the weight; and in one instance I used three ounces to a pint decoction, before the desired effect took place. I consider the Foxglove thus given, as the most certain diuretic I know, nor do its diuretic effects depend merely upon the nausea it produces, for in cases where squill and ipecac. have been so given as to keep up a nausea several days together, and the flow of urine not taken place, I have found the Foxglove to succeed; and I have, in more than one instance, given the Foxglove in smaller and more distant doses, so that the flow of urine has taken place without any sensible affection of the stomach; but in general I give it in the manner first mentioned, and order one dose to be taken after the sickness commences. I then omit all medicines, except those of the cordial kind are wanted, during the space of three, four, or five days. By this time the nausea abates, and the appetite becomes better than it was before. Sometimes the brain is considerably affected by the medicine, and indistinct vision ensues; but I have never yet found any permanent bad effects from it."—

"I use it in the Ascites, Anasarca, and Hydrops Pectoris; and so far as the removal of the water will contribute to cure the patient, so far may be expected from this medicine: but I wish it not to be tried in ascites of female patients, believing that many of these cases are dropsies of the ovaria; and no sensible man will ever expect to see these encysted fluids removed by any medicine."

"I have often been obliged to evacuate the water repeatedly in the same patient, by repeating the decoction; but then this has been at such distances of time as to allow of the interference of other medicines and a proper regimen, so that the patient obtains in the end a perfect cure. In these cases the decoction becomes at length so very disagreeable, that a much smaller quantity will produce the effect, and I often find it necessary to alter its taste by the addition of Aq. Cinnam. sp. or Aq. Juniper. composita."

"I allow, and indeed enjoin my patients to drink very plentifully of small liquors through the whole course of the cure; and sometimes, where the evacuations have been very sudden, I have found a bandage as necessary as in the use of the trochar."—

Early in the year 1779, a number of dropsical cases offered themselves to my attention, the consequences of the scarlet fever and sore throat which had raged so very generally amongst us in the preceding year. Some of these had been cured by squills or other diuretics, and relapsed; in others, the dropsy did not appear for several weeks after the original disease had ceased: but I am not able to mention many particulars, having omitted to make notes. This, however, is the less to be regretted, as the symptoms in all were very much alike, and they were all without an exception cured by the Foxglove.

This last circumstance encouraged me to use the medicine more frequently than I had done heretofore, and the increase of practice had taught me to improve the management of it.

In February 1779, my friend, Dr. Stokes, communicated to the Medical Society at Edinburgh the result of my experience of the Foxglove; and, in a letter addressed to me in November following, he says, "Dr. Hope, in consequence of my mentioning its use to my friend, Dr. Broughton, has tried the Foxglove in the Infirmary with success." Dr. Stokes also tells me that Dr. Hamilton cured Dropsies with it in the year 1781.

I am informed by my very worthy friend Dr. Duncan, that Dr. Hamilton, who learnt its use from Dr. Hope, has employed it very frequently in the Hospital at Edinburgh. Dr. Duncan also tells me, that the late very ingenious and accomplished Mr. Charles Darwin, informed him of its being used by his father and myself, in cases of Hydrothorax, and that he has ever since mentioned it in his lectures, and sometimes employed it in his practice.

At length, in the year 1783, it appeared in the new edition of the Edinburgh Pharmacopœia, into which, I am told, it was received in consequence of the recommendation of Dr. Hope. But from which, I am satisfied, it will be again very soon rejected, if it should continue to be exhibited in the unrestrained manner in which it has heretofore been used at Edinburgh, and in the enormous doses in which it is now directed in London.

In the following cases the reader will find other diseases besides dropsies; particularly several cases of consumption. I was induced to try it in these, from being told, that it was much used in the West of England, in the Phthisis Pulmonalis, by the common people. In this disease, however, in my hands, it has done but little service, and yet I am disposed to wish it a further trial, for in a copy of Parkinson's Herbal, which I saw about two years ago, I found the following manuscript note at the article Digitalis, written, I believe, by a Mr. Saunders, who practised for many years with great reputation as a surgeon and apothecary at Stourbridge, in Worcestershire.

"Consumptions are cured infallibly by weak decoction of Foxglove leaves in water, or wine and water, and drank for constant drink. Or take of the juice of the herb and flowers, clarify it, and make a fine syrup with honey, of which take three spoonfuls thrice in a day, at physical hours. The use of these two things of late has done, in consumptive cases, great wonders. But be cautious of its use, for it is of a vomiting nature. In these things begin sparingly, and increase the dose as the patient's strength will bear, least, instead of a sovereign medicine, you do real damage by this infusion or syrup."

The precautions annexed to his encomiums of this medicine, lead one to think that he has spoken from his own proper experience.

I have lately been told, that a person in the neighbourhood of Warwick, possesses a famous family receipt for the dropsy, in which the Foxglove is the active medicine; and a lady from the western part of Yorkshire assures me, that the people in her country often cure themselves of dropsical complaints by drinking Foxglove tea. In confirmation of this, I recollect about two years ago being desired to visit a travelling Yorkshire tradesman. I found him incessantly vomiting, his vision indistinct, his pulse forty in a minute. Upon enquiry it came out, that his wife had stewed a large handful of green Foxglove leaves in half a pint of water, and given him the liquor, which he drank at one draught, in order to cure him of an asthmatic affection. This good woman knew the medicine of her country, but not the dose of it, for her husband narrowly escaped with his life.

It is probable that this rude mode of exhibiting the Foxglove has been more general than I am at present aware of; but it is wonderful that no author seems to have been acquainted with its effects as a diuretic.

CASES, In which the Digitalis was given by the Direction of the Author

1775.

It was in the course of this year that I began to use the Digitalis in dropsical cases. The patients were such as applied at my house for advice gratis. I cannot pretend to charge my memory with particular cases, or particular effects, and I had not leisure to make notes. Upon the whole, however, it may be concluded, that the medicine was found useful, or I should not have continued to employ it.

CASE I.

December 8th. A man about fifty years of age, who had formerly been a builder, but was now much reduced in his circumstances, complained to me of an asthma which first attacked him about the latter end of autumn. His breath was very short, his countenance was sunken, his belly large; and, upon examination, a fluctuation in it was very perceptible. His urine for some time past had been small in quantity. I directed a decoction of Fol. Digital. recent. which made him very sick, the sickness recurring at intervals for several days, during which time he made a large quantity of water. His breath gradually drew easier, his belly subsided, and in about ten days he began to eat with a keen appetite. He afterwards took steel and bitters.

1776.
CASE II.

January 14th. A poor man labouring under an ascites and anasarca, was directed to take a decoction of Digitalis every four hours. It purged him smartly, but did not relieve him. An opiate was now ordered with each dose of the medicine, which then acted upon the kidneys very freely, and he soon lost all his complaints.

CASE III.

March 15th. A poor boy, about nine years of age, was brought for my advice. His countenance was pale, his pulse quick and feeble, his body greatly emaciated, except his belly, which was very large, and, upon examination, contained a fluid. The case had been considered as arising from worms. He was directed to take the decoction of Digitalis night and morning. It operated as a diuretic, never made him sick, and he got well without any other medicine.

CASE IV.

July 25th. Mrs. H——, of A——, near N——, between forty and fifty years of age, a few weeks ago, after some previous indisposition, was attacked by a severe cold shivering fit, succeeded by fever; great pain in her left side, shortness of breath, perpetual cough, and, after some days, copious expectoration. On the 4th of June, Dr. Darwin, was called to her. I have not heard what was then done for her, but, between the 15th of June, and 25th of July, the Doctor, at his different visits, gave her various medicines of the deobstruent, tonic, antispasmodic, diuretic, and evacuant kinds.

On the 25th of July I was desired to meet Dr. Darwin at the lady's house. I found her nearly in a state of suffocation; her pulse extremely weak and irregular, her breath very short and laborious, her countenance sunk, her arms of a leaden colour, clammy and cold. She could not lye down in bed, and had neither strength nor appetite, but was extremely thirsty. Her stomach, legs, and thighs were greatly swollen; her urine very small in quantity, not more than a spoonful at a time, and that very seldom. It had been proposed to scarify her legs, but the proposition was not acceded to.

She had experienced no relief from any means that had been used, except from ipecacoanha vomits; the dose of which had been gradually increased from 15 to 40 grains, but such was the insensible state of her stomach for the last few days, that even those very large doses failed to make her sick, and consequently purged her. In this situation of things I knew of nothing likely to avail us, except the Digitalis: but this I hesitated to propose, from an apprehension that little could be expected from any thing; that an unfavourable termination would tend to discredit a medicine which promised to be of great benefit to mankind, and I might be censured for a prescription which could not be countenanced by the experience of any other regular practitioner. But these considerations soon gave way to the desire of preserving the life of this valuable woman, and accordingly I proposed the Digitalis to be tried; adding, that I sometimes had found it to succeed when other, even the most judicious methods, had failed. Dr. Darwin very politely, acceded immediately to my proposition, and, as he had never seen it given, left the preparation and the dose to my direction. We therefore prescribed as follows:

R. Fol. Digital. purp. recent. ʒiv. coque ex

Aq. fontan. puræ ℔ss ad ℔i. et cola.

R. Decoct. Digital. ʒiss.

Aq. Nuc. Moschat. ʒii. M. fiat. haust. 2dis horis sumend.

The patient took five of these draughts, which made her very sick, and acted very powerfully upon the kidneys, for within the first twenty-four hours she made upwards of eight quarts of water. The sense of fulness and oppression across her stomach was greatly diminished, her breath was eased, her pulse became more full and more regular, and the swellings of her legs subsided.

26th. Our patient being thus snatched from impending destruction, Dr. Darwin proposed to give her a decoction of pareira brava and guiacum shavings, with pills of myrrh and white vitriol; and, if costive, a pill with calomel and aloes. To these propositions I gave a ready assent.

30th. This day Dr. Darwin saw her, and directed a continuation of the medicines last prescribed.

August 1st. I found the patient perfectly free from every appearance of dropsy, her breath quite easy, her appetite much improved, but still very weak. Having some suspicion of a diseased liver, I directed pills of soap, rhubarb, tartar of vitriol, and calomel to be taken twice a day, with a neutral saline draught.

9th. We visited our patient together, and repeated the draughts directed on the 26th of June, with the addition of tincture of bark, and also ordered pills of aloes, guiacum, and sal martis to be taken if costive.

September 10th. From this time the management of the case fell entirely under my direction, and perceiving symptoms of effusion going forwards, I desired that a solution of merc. subl. corr. might be given twice a day.

19th. The increase of the dropsical symptoms now made it necessary to repeat the Digitalis. The dried leaves were used in infusion, and the water was presently evacuated, as before.

It is now almost nine years since the Digitalis was first prescribed for this lady, and notwithstanding I have tried every preventive method I could devise, the dropsy still continues to recur at times; but is never allowed to increase so as to cause much distress, for she occasionally takes the infusion and relieves herself whenever she chooses. Since the first exhibition of that medicine, very small doses have been always found sufficient to promote the flow of urine.

I have been more particular in the narrative of this case, partly because Dr. Darwin has related it rather imperfectly in the notes to his son's posthumous publication, trusting, I imagine, to memory, and partly because it was a case which gave rise to a very general use of the medicine in that part of Shropshire.

CASE V.

December 10th. Mr. L——, Æt. 35. Ascites and anasarca, the consequence of very intemperate living. After trying squill and other medicines to no purpose, I directed a decoction of the Fol. Digital. recent. six drams to a pint; an eighth part to be taken every fourth hour. This made him sick, and produced a copious flow of urine, but not enough to remove all the dropsical symptoms. After a fortnight a stronger decoction was ordered, and, upon a third trial, as the winter advanced, it became necessary to use four ounces to the pint decoction; and thus he got free from all his complaints.

In October 1777, in consequence of having pursued his intemperate mode of living, his dropsy returned, accompanied by evident marks of diseased viscera. A decoction of two drams of Fol. Digital. siccat. to a pint, once more removed the dropsy. He took a wine glass full thrice a day.

In January 1778, I was desired to visit him again. I found he had gone on in his usual intemperate life, his countenance jaundiced, and the dropsy coming on apace. After giving some deobstruent medicines, I again directed the Digitalis, which again emptied the water; but he did not survive many weeks.

1777.

CASE VI.

February—. Mrs. M——, Æt. 45. Ascites and anasarca, but not much otherwise diseased, and well enough to walk about the house, and see after her family affairs. I thought this a fair case for a trial of the Digitalis, and therefore directed a decoction of the fresh leaves, the stock of dried ones being exhausted. About a week afterwards, calling to see my patient, I was informed that she was dead; that the third day after my first visit she suddenly fell down, and expired. Upon enquiry I found she had not taken any of the medicine; for the snow had lain so deep upon the ground, that the apothecary had not been able to procure it. Had the medicine been given in a case seemingly so favourable as this, and had the patient died under its use, is it not probable that the death would have been attributed to it?

CASE VII.

February 11th. Mr. E——, of W——, Æt. 61. Hydrothorax, ascites and anasarca, consequences of hard drinking. He had been attended for some time by a physician in his neighbourhood, who had treated his case with the usual remedies, but without affording him any relief; nor could I expect to succeed better by any other medicine than the Digitalis. The dried leaves were not to be had; and the green ones at this season being very uncertain in their strength, I ordered four ounces of the roots in a pint decoction, and directed three spoonfuls to be given every fourth hour, until it either excited nausea, or a free discharge of urine; both these effects took place nearly at the same time: he made a large quantity of water, the swellings subsided very considerably, and his breath became easy. Eight days afterwards he began upon a course of bitters and deobstruents. The dropsical symptoms soon increased again, but he had suffered so much from the severity of the sickness before, that he was neither willing to take, nor I to give the same medicine again.

Perhaps this patient might have been saved, if I had been well acquainted with the management and real doses of the medicine, which was certainly in this instance made very much too strong; and notwithstanding the caution to stop the further exhibition when certain effects should take place, it seems the quantity previously swallowed was sufficient to distress him exceedingly.

CASE VIII.

March 11th. Mrs. H——, Æt. 32. A few days after a tedious labour, had her legs and thighs swelled to a very great degree; pale and semi-transparent, with pain in both groins. After a purge of calomel and rhubarb, ung. merc. was ordered to be rubbed upon the groins, and the following decoction was directed:

R. Fol. Digital. purp. recent. ℥ii.

Aq. puræ. ℔i. coque ad ℔ss et colatur. adde.

Aq. cinn. sp. ℥iv. M. capiat. cyath. vinos. parv. bis quotidie.

The decoction presently increased the secretion of urine, and abated the distension of the legs: in a fortnight the swelling was gone; but some days after leaving her bed, her legs swelled again about the ancles, which was removed by another bottle of the decoction on the 21st of April.

CASE IX.

March 29th. Mr. G——, Æt. 47. Very much deformed; asthma of several years continuance, but now dropsical to a great degree. Took several medicines without relief, and then tried the Digitalis, but with no better success.

CASE X.

April 10th. G—G——, Æt. 70. Asthma and anasarca. Took a decoction of the fresh leaves of the Digitalis, which produced violent sickness, but no immediate evacuation of water. After the sickness had ceased altogether, the urine began to flow copiously, and he was cured.

CASE XI.

July 10th. Mr. M—— of T——, Æt. 54. A very hard drinker; had been affected since November last with ascites and anasarca, for which he had taken several medicines without benefit. A decoction of the recent leaves of the Digitalis was then directed, an ounce and half to a pint, one eighth of which I ordered to be given every fourth hour. A few doses brought on great nausea, indistinct vision, and a great flow of urine, so as presently to empty him of all the dropsical water. Indeed the evacuation was so rapid and so complete, that it became necessary to apply a bandage round the belly, and to support him with cordials.

In something more than a year and a half, his dropsy returned, but the Digitalis did not then succeed to our wishes. In August, 1779, he was tapped, and lived afterwards only about five weeks.

For more particulars, see the extract of a letter from Mr. Lyon.

CASE XII.

September 12th. Miss C—— of T——, Æt 48. An ovarium dropsy, and anasarcous legs and thighs. For three months in the beginning of this year she had been under the care of Dr. Darwin, who at different times had given her blue vitriol, elaterium, and calomel; decoction of pareira brava, and guiacum wood, with tincture of cantharides; oxymel of squills, decoction of parsley roots, &c. Finding no relief, she discontinued the use of medicines, until the urgency of her symptoms induced her to ask my advice about the end of August. She was greatly emaciated, and had almost a total loss of appetite. I first tried small doses of Merc. sublim. corr. in solution, with decoction of burdock roots, and blisters to the thighs. No advantage attending the use of this plan, I directed a decoction of Fol. Digit. a dram and half to a pint; one ounce to be taken twice a day. It presently reduced the anasarcous swellings, but made no alteration in the distension of the abdomen.

CASE XIII.

October 9th. Mrs. B——, Æt. 40. An ovarium dropsy. Took a decoction of Digitalis without effect. Her life was preserved for some years by repeated tapping.

1778.
CASE XIV.

February 8th. Mr. R—— of K——. Had formerly suffered much from gout, and lived very intemperately. Jaundiced countenance; ascites; legs and thighs greatly swollen; appetite none; extremely weak; confined to his bed. Had taken many medicines from his apothecary without advantage. I ordered him decoction of Digitalis, and a cordial; but he survived only a few days.

CASE XV.

March 13th. Mr. M——, Æt. 54. A thorax greatly deformed; asthma through the winter, succeeded by dropsy in belly and legs. Pulse very small; face leaden coloured; cough almost continual. Decoction of seneka was directed, and small doses of Dover's powder at night.

17th. Gum-ammoniac and squill, with elixir paregor. at night.—26th, Squill and decoction of seneka.—30th, His complaints still increasing, decoction of Digitalis was then directed, which relieved him in a few days; but his complaints returned again, and he died in the month of June.

CASE XVI.

August 18th. Mr. B——, Æt. 33. Pulmonary consumption and dropsy. The Digitalis, and that failing, other diuretics were used, in hopes of gaining some relief from the distress occasioned by the dropsical symptoms; but none of them were effectual. He was then attended by another physician, and died in about two months.

CASE XVII.

September 21st. Mrs. M—— W—— G——, Æt. 50. An ovarium dropsy. She took half a pint of Infus. Digitalis, which made her sick, but did not increase the quantity of urine. She was afterwards relieved by tapping.

CASE XVIII.

October 28th. R—— W——, Æt. 33. Ascites and universal anasarca; countenance quite pale and bloated; appetite none, and the little food he forces down is generally rejected.

R. Fol. Digit. purp. siccat. ʒiii.

Aq. bull. ℔i. digere per horas duas, et colat. adde aq. junip. comp. ʒiii.

He was directed to take one ounce of this infusion every two hours until it should make him sick. This was on Wednesday. The fifth dose made him vomit. On Thursday afternoon he vomited again very freely, without having taken any more of the medicine. On Friday and Saturday he made more water than he had done for a week before, and the swellings of his face and body were considerably abated. He was directed to omit all medicine so long as the urine continued to flow freely, and also to keep an account of the quantity he made in twenty-four hours.

These were his reports:

October	31st.	Saturday,	5 half pints.
November	1st.	Sunday,	6
	2d.	Monday,	8
	3d.	Tuesday,	8
	4th.	Wednesday,	7
	5th.	Thursday,	8

On Wednesday he began to purge, and the purging still continues, but his appetite is better than he has known it for a long time. No swelling remains but about his ancles, extending at night half way up his legs.

Omit all medicines at present.

| | 7th. | Saturday, | 7½ half pints. |

8th.	Sunday,	8
9th.	Monday,	6¾
10th.	Tuesday,	6½
11th.	Wednesday,	6
12th.	Thursday,	6¼

On Tuesday the 17th, some swelling still remained about his ancles, but he was in every other respect perfectly well.

He took a few more doses of the infusion, and no other medicine.

CASE XIX.

December 8th. W—— B——, Æt. 60. A hard drinker. Diseased viscera; ascites and anasarca. An infusion of Digitalis was directed, but it had no other effect than to make him sick.

1779.

In the beginning of this year we had many dropsies in children, who had suffered from the Scarlatina Anginosa; they all yielded very readily to the Digitalis, but in some the medicine purged, and then it did not prove diuretic, nor did it remove the dropsy until opium was joined with it, so as to prevent it purging.—I did not keep notes of these cases, but I do not recollect a single instance in which the Digitalis failed to effect a cure.

CASE XX.

January 1st. Mr. H——. Hydrops Pectoris; legs and thighs prodigiously anasarcous; a very distressing sense of fulness and tightness across his stomach; urine in small quantity; pulse intermitting; breath very short.

He had taken various medicines, and been blistered, but without relief. His complaints continuing to increase, I directed an infusion of Digitalis, which made him very sick; acted powerfully as a diuretic, and removed all his symptoms.

About three months afterwards he was out upon a journey, and, after taking cold, was suddenly seized with difficulty of breathing, and violent palpitation of his heart: he sent for me, and I ordered the infusion as before, which very soon removed his complaints. He is now active and well; but, whenever he takes cold, finds some return of difficult breathing, which he soon removes by a dose or two of the infusion.

CASE XXI.

January 5th. Mrs. M——, Æt. 69. Hydrothorax, (called asthma) ascites and anasarca. I directed an infusion of Fol. Digital. siccat. three drams to a pint; a small wine glass to be taken every third or fourth hour. It made her violently sick, acted powerfully as a diuretic, set her breath perfectly at liberty, and carried off the swelling of her legs; when she was nearly emptied, she became so languid, that I thought it necessary to order cordials, and a large blister to her back. Mr. Ward, who attended as her apothecary, tells me she had some return of her asthma in June and October following, which was each time removed by the same medicine.

CASE XXII.

January 11th. Mr. H——, Æt. 59. Ascites and general anasarca. A large corpulent man, and a hard drinker: he had repeatedly suffered under complaints of this kind, but had been always relieved by the judicious assistance of Dr. Ash. In the present instance, however, not finding relief as usual from the prescriptions of my worthy friend, he sent for me; after examining into his situation, and informing myself what had been done to relieve him, I was satisfied that the Digitalis was the only medicine from which I had any thing to hope. It was therefore directed; but another patient requiring my assistance at a distance from town, I desired he would not begin the medicine before I returned, which would be early on the third day; for I was well aware of the difficulties before me, and that he would inevitably sink under too rapid an evacuation of the water. On my return I was informed, that the preceding evening, as he sat on his chair, his head sunk upon his breast, and he died.

This case, as well as case VI. is mentioned with a view to demonstrate to younger practitioners, how sudden and unexpected the deaths of dropsical patients sometimes happen, and how cautious we should be in assigning causes for effects.

CASE XXIII.

August 31st. Mr. C——, Æt. 57. Diseased viscera, jaundice, ascites and anasarca. After trying calomel, saline draughts, jallap purges, chrystals of tartar, pills of gum ammoniac, squills, and soap, sal succini, eleterium, &c. infusion of Digitalis was directed, which removed all his urgent symptoms, and he recovered a pretty good state of health.

CASE XXIV.

September 11th. I was desired to visit Mr. L——, Æt. 63; a middle sized man; rather thin; not habitually intemperate; found him in bed, where he had been for three days. He was in a state of furious insanity, and had been gradually losing his reason for ten days before, but was not outrageous the first week; his apothecary had given him ten grains of emetic tartar, a dram of ipecacoanha, and an ounce of tincture of jallap, in the space of a few hours, which scarcely made him sick, and only occasioned a stool or two; upon enquiring into the usual state of his health, I was told that he had been troubled with some difficulty of breathing for thirty years past, but for the nine last years this complaint had increased, so that he was often obliged to sit up the greater part of the night; and, for the last year, the sense of suffocation was so great, when he lay down, that he often sat up for a week together. His father died of an asthma before he was fifty. A few years ago, at an election, where he drank more than usual, his head was affected as now, but in a slighter degree, and his asthmatic symptoms vanished; and now, notwithstanding he has been several days in bed, he feels not the least difficulty in breathing.

Apprehending that the insanity might be owing to the same cause which had heretofore occasioned the asthma, and that this cause was water; I ordered a decoction of the Fol. siccat Digital, three drams to half a pint; three spoonfuls to be taken every third hour: the fourth dose made him sick; the medicine was then stopped; the sickness continued at intervals, more or less, for four days, during which time he made a great quantity of water, and gradually became more rational. On the fifth day his appetite began to return, and the sickness ceased, but the flow of urine still continued.

A week afterwards I saw him again, and examined him particularly; his head was then perfectly rational, appetite very good, breath quite easy, permitting him to lie down in bed without inconvenience, makes plenty of water, coughs a little, and expectorates freely. He took no other medicine, except a little rhubarb when costive.

CASE XXV.

September 15th. Mr. J. R——, Æt. 50. Subject to an asthmatical complaint for more than twenty years, but was this year much worse than usual, and symptoms of dropsy appeared. In July he took G. ammon. squill and seneka, with infus. amarum and fossil alkaly. In August, infusum amar. with vin. chalyb. and at bed-time pil. styr. and squill. His complaints increasing, the squill was pushed as far as could be borne, but without any good effect. September 15th, an infusion of Digitalis was directed, but he died the next morning.

CASE XXVI.

September 18th. Mrs. R——, Æt. 30. After a severe child-bearing, found both her legs and thighs swelled to the utmost stretch of the skin. They looked pale, and almost transparent. The case being similar to that related at No. VIII. I determined upon a similar method of treatment; but as this patient had an inflammatory sore throat also, I wished to get that removed first, and in three or four days it was done. I then directed an infusion of Digitalis, which soon increased the urinary secretion, and reduced the swellings, without any disturbance of her stomach.

A few days after quitting her bed and coming down stairs, some degree of swelling in her legs returned, which was removed by calomel, an opening electuary, and the application of rollers.

CASE XXVII.

October 7th. Mr. F——, a little man, with a spine and thorax greatly deformed; for more than a year past had complained of difficult respiration, and a sense of fulness about his stomach; these complaints increasing, his abdomen gradually enlarged, and a fluctuation in it became perceptible. He had no anasarca, no appearance of diseased viscera, and no great paucity of urine. Purges and diuretics of different kinds affording him no relief, my assistance was desired. After trying squill medicines without effect, he was ordered to take Pulv. fol. Digital. in small doses. These producing no sensible effect, the doses were gradually increased until nausea was excited; but there was no alteration in the quantity of urine, and consequently no relief to his complaints. I then advised tapping, but he would not hear of it; however, the distress occasioned by the increasing fulness of his belly at length compelled him to submit to the operation on the 20th of November. It was necessary to draw off the water again upon the following days:

	December the	8th.
	— —	27th.
1780.	February the	4th.
	— —	23d.
	March the	9th.

During the intervals, no method I could think of was omitted to prevent the return of the disease, but nothing seemed to avail. In the operation of February 23d, his strength was so much reduced, that the water was not entirely removed; and on the 9th of March, before his belly was half emptied, notwithstanding the most judicious application of bandage, his debility was so great, that it was judged prudent to stop. After being placed in bed, the faintness and sickness continued; severe rigors ensued, and violent vomiting; these vomitings continued through the night, and in the intervals he lay in a state nearly approaching to syncope. The next day I found him with nearly the same symptoms, but remarked that the quantity of fluid he had thrown up was very much more than what he had taken, and that his abdomen was considerably fallen; in the course of two or three days more, he discharged the whole of the effused fluid; his strength and appetite gradually returned, and he was in all respects much better than he had been before the last operation.

Some time afterwards, his belly began to fill again, and he again applied to me; upon an accurate examination, I judged the quantity of fluid might then be about four or five quarts. Nature had pointed out the true method of cure in this case; I therefore ordered him to bed, and directed ipecacoanha vomits to be given night and morning: in two or three days the whole of the water was removed by vomiting, for he never purged, nor was the quantity of his urine increased; his appetite and strength gradually returned; he never had any further relapse, and is now an active healthy man. I must leave the reader to make his own reflections on this singular case.

1780.
CASE XXVIII.

January 11th. Captain V——, Æt. 42. Had suffered much from residing in hot climates, and drinking very freely, particularly rum in large quantity. He had tried many physicians before I saw him, but nothing relieved him. I found him greatly emaciated, his countenance of a brownish yellow; no appetite, extremely low, distressing fulness across his stomach; legs and thighs greatly swollen; pulse quick, and very feeble; urine in small quantity. As he had evidently only a few days to live, I ordered him nothing but a solution of sal diureticus in cinnamon water, slightly acidulated with syrup of lemons. This medicine effecting no change, and his symptoms becoming daily more distressing, I directed an infusion of Digitalis. A few doses occasioned a copious flow of urine, without sickness or any other disturbance. The medicine was discontinued; and the next day the urine continuing to be secreted very plentifully, he lost his most distressing complaints, was in great spirits, and ate a pretty good dinner. In the evening, as he was conversing chearfully with some friends, he stooped forwards, fell from his chair, and died instantly. Had he been in bed, I think there is reason to believe this fatal syncope, if such it was, would not have happened.

CASE XXIX.

February 6th. Mr. H——, Æt. 63. A corpulent man; had suffered much from gout, which for the last year or two had formed very imperfectly. He had now symptoms of water in his chest, his belly and his legs. An infusion of Digitalis removed these complaints, and after being confined for the greater part of the winter, he was well enough to get abroad again. In the course of a month the dropsical symptoms returned, and were again removed by the same medicine. Bitters and tonics were now occasionally prescribed, but his debility gradually increased, and he died some time afterwards; but the dropsy never returned.

CASE XXX.

February 17th. Mr. D——, Æt. 50. Ascites and anasarca, with symptoms of phthisis. He had been a very hard drinker. The infusum Digitalis removed his dropsical symptoms, and he was sufficiently recovered to take a journey; but as the spring advanced, the consumptive symptoms increased, and he died soon afterwards, perfectly emaciated.

CASE XXXI.

March 5th. I was desired to visit Mrs. H——, a very delicate woman, who after a severe lying-in, had her legs and thighs swollen to a very great degree; pale and semi-transparent. I found her extremely faint, her pulse very small and slow; vomiting violently, and frequently purging. She was attended by a gentleman who had seen me give the Digitalis in a similar case of swelled legs after a lying-in (see Case XXVI.) about six months before. He had not considered that this patient was delicate, the other robust; nor had he attended to stop the exhibition of the medicine when its effects began to take place. The great distress of her situation was evidently owing to the imprudent and unlimited use of the Digitalis. I was very apprehensive for her safety; ordered her cordials and volatiles; a free supply of wine, chamomile tea with brandy for common drink, and blisters. The next day the situation of things was much the same, but with all this disturbance no increased secretion of urine. The same methods were continued; an opiate ordered at night, and liniment. volatile upon flannel applied to the groins, as she now complained of great pain in those parts. The third day the nausea was less urgent, the vomitings less frequent, the pulse not so slow. Camphorated spirit, with caustic volatile alkaly, was applied to the stomach, emulsion given for common drink, and the same medicines repeated. From this time, the intervals became gradually longer between the fits of vomiting, the flow of urine increased, the swellings subsided, the appetite returned, and she recovered perfectly.

CASE XXXII.

March 16th. Mr. D——, Æt. 70. A paralytic stroke had for some weeks past impaired the use of his left side, and he complained much of his breath, and of a straitness across his stomach; at length, an anasarca and ascites appearing, I had no doubt as to the cause of the former symptoms; but, upon account of his advanced age, and the paralytic affection, I hesitated to give the Digitalis, and therefore tried the other usual modes of practice, until at length his breath would not permit him to lie down in bed, and his other symptoms increased so rapidly as to threaten a speedy dissolution. In this dilemma I ventured to prescribe an infusion of the Fol. siccat. Digital. which presently excited a copious flow of urine, and made him very sick; a strong infusion of chamomile flowers, with brandy, relieved the sickness, but the diuretic effects of the Digitalis continuing, his dropsy was removed, and his breathing became easy. The palsy remained nearly in the same state. He lived until August 1782, and without any return of the dropsy.

CASE XXXIII.

March 18th. Miss S——, Æt. 5. Hydrocephalus internus. As the case did not yield to calomel, when matters were nearly advanced to extremities, it occurred to me to try the Infusum Digitalis; a few doses of which were given, but had no sensible effect.

CASE XXXIV.

March 19th. A young lady, soon after the birth of an illegitimate child, became insane. After being near a month under my care, swellings of her legs, which at first had been attributed to weakness, extended to her thighs and belly; her urine became foul, and small in quantity, and the insanity remained nearly the same. As it had been very difficult to procure evacuations by any means, I ordered half an ounce of Fol. Digital. siccat. in a pint infusion, and directed two spoonfuls to be given every two hours: this had the desired effect; the dropsy and the insanity disappeared together, and she had afterwards no other medicine but some aperient pills to take occasionally.

CASE XXXV.

April 12th. Mr. R——, Æt. 32. For the last three or four years had had more or less of what was considered as asthma;—it appeared to me Hydrothorax. I directed an infusion of Digitalis, which presently removed his complaints. In June following he had a relapse, and took two grains of the Pulv. fol. Digit. three times a day, which cured him after taking forty grains, and he has never had a return.

CASE XXXVI.

May 15th. Mrs. H——, Æt. 40. A spasmodic asthma, attended with symptoms of effusion. An infusion of Digitalis relieved her very considerably, and she lived four years afterwards without any relapse.

CASE XXXVII.

May 26th. R—— B——, Æt. 12. Scrophulous, consumptive, and at length anasarcous. Took Infus. Digital. without advantage. Died the July following.

CASE XXXVIII.

June 4th. Mrs. S——, of W——, Æt 49. Ascites and anasarca. Had taken many medicines; first from her apothecary, afterwards by the direction of a very judicious and very celebrated physician, but nothing retarded the increase of the dropsy. I first saw her along with the physician mentioned above, on the 14th of May; we directed an electuary of chrystals of tartar, and Seltzer water for common drink; this plan failing, as others had done before, we ordered the Infus. Digital. which in a few days nearly removed the dropsy. I then left her to the care of her physician; but her constitution was too much impaired to admit of restoration to health, and I understand she died a few weeks afterwards.

CASE XXXIX.

June 13th. Mr. P——, Æt. 35. A very hard drinker, was attacked with a severe hæmoptoe, which was followed by ascites and anasarca. He had every appearance of diseased viscera, and his urine was small in quantity. The powder and the infusion of Digitalis were given at different times, but without the desired effect. Other medicines were tried, but in vain. Tapping prolonged his existence a few weeks, and he died early in the following autumn.

CASE XL.

June 27th. Mr. W——, Æt. 37. An apparently asthmatic affection, gradually increasing for three or four years, which not yielding to the usual remedies, he took the infusion of Digitalis. Two or three doses made him very sick; but he thought his breathing relieved. After one week he took it again, and was so much better as to want no other medicine.

In the course of the following winter he became hectic, and died consumptive about a year afterwards.

CASE XLI.

July 6th. Mr. E——, Æt. 57. Hydrothorax and anasarca; his breath so short that he could not lie down. After a trial of squill, fixed alkaly, and dulcified spirit of nitre, I directed Pulv. Digital. gr. 2, thrice a day. In four days he was able to come down stairs; in three days more no appearance of disease remained; and under the use of aromatics and small doses of opium, he soon recovered his strength.

CASE XLII.

July 7th. Miss H—— of T——, Æt. 39. In the last stage of a phthisis pulmonalis became dropsical. She took the Digitalis without being relieved.

CASE XLIII.

July 9th. Mrs. F——, Æt. 70. A chearful, strong, healthy woman; but for a few years back had experienced a degree of difficult breathing when in exercise. In the course of the last year her legs swelled, and she felt great fulness about her stomach. These symptoms continued increasing very fast, notwithstanding several attempts made by a very judicious apothecary to relieve her. The more regular practitioner failing, she had recourse to a quack, who I believe plied her very powerfully with Daphne laureola, or some drastic purge of that kind. I found her greatly reduced in strength, her belly and lower extremities swollen to an amazing size, her urine small in quantity, and her appetite greatly impaired. For the first fortnight of my attendance blisters were applied, solution of fixed alkaly, decoction of seneka with vitriolic æther, chrystals of tartar, squill and cordial medicines were successively exhibited, but with no advantage. I then directed Pulv. Fol. Digital. two grains every four hours. After taking eighteen grains, the urine began to increase. The medicine was then stopped. The discharge of urine continued to increase, and in five or six days the whole of the dropsical water passed off, without any disturbance to the stomach or bowels. As the distension of the belly had been very great, a swathe was applied, and drawn gradually tighter as the water was evacuated. As no pains were spared to prevent the return of the dropsy, and as the best means I could devise proved unequal to my wishes, both in this and in some other cases, I shall take the liberty to point out the methods I tried at different times in as concise a manner as possible, for the knowledge of what will not do, may sometimes assist us to discover what will.

1780.

July 18th. Infusum amarum, steel, Seltzer water.

September 22d. Neutral saline draughts, with tinct. canthar.

26th. Pills of soap, garlic and millepedes.

30th. The same pills, with infusum amarum.

October 11th. Pills of aloes, assafetida, and sal martis, in the day-time, and mercury rubbed down, at night.

December 21st. The accumulation of water now required a repetition of the Digitalis. It was directed in infusion, a dram and half to eight ounces, and an ounce and half given every fourth hour, until its effects began to appear. The water was soon carried off.

30th. Sal diuretic. twice a day. To eat preserved garlic frequently.

1781.

February 1st. Pills of calomel, squill and gum ammoniac.

3d. Infusion of Digitalis repeated, and after the water was carried off, Dover's powder was tried as a sudorific.

March 18th. Infus. Digital. repeated.

26th. Pills of sal martis and aromatic species, with infusum amarum.

May 5th. Being feverish; James's powder and saline draughts.

10th. Laudanum every night, and an opening tincture to obviate costiveness.

24th. Infus. Digitalis, one ounce only every fourth hour, which soon procured a perfect evacuation of the water.

August 11th. Infus. Digitalis.

October 19th. An emetic, and fol. Cicut. pulv. ten grains every six hours.

November 8th. A mercurial bolus at bed-time.

16th. Infus. Digitalis.

December 23d. An emetic—Pills of seneka and gum ammoniac—Vitriolic acid in every thing she drinks.

25th. Squill united to small doses of opium.

1782.

January 2d. A troublesome cough—Syrup of garlic and oxymel of squills. A blister to the back.

4th. Tincture of cantharides and paregoric elixir.

28th. Infus. Digitalis, half an ounce every morning, and one ounce every night, was now sufficient to empty her.

March 26th. Infus. Digitalis; and when emptied, vitriol of copper twice a day.

April 1st. A cordial mixture for occasional use.

Two months afterwards a purging came on, which every now and then returned, inducing great weakness—her appetite failed, and she died in July.

INTERVALS.

- From July 9th, 1780, to December 21st, 171 days.
- From December 21st to February 3d, 1781, 34 days.
- From February 3d to March 18th, 44 days.
- From March 18th to May 24th, 66 days.
- From May 24th to August 11th, 79 days.
- From August 11th to November 16th, 98 days.
- From November 16th to January 28th, 1782, 74 days.
- From January 28th to March 26th, 57 days.

None of the accumulations of water were at all equal to that which existed when I first saw her, for finding so easy a mode of relief, she became impatient under a small degree of pressure, and often insisted upon taking her medicine sooner than I thought it necessary. After the 26th of March the degree of effusion was inconsiderable, and at the time of her death very trifling, being probably carried off by the diarrhœa.

CASE XLIV.

July 12th. Mr. H——, of A——, Æt. 60. In the last stage of a life hurried to a termination by free living, dropsical symptoms became the most distressing. He wished to take the Digitalis. It was given, but afforded no relief.

CASE XLV.

July 13th. Mr. S——, Æt. 49. Asthma, or rather hydrothorax, anasarca, and symptoms of a diseased liver. He was directed to take two grains of Pulv. fol. Digital. every two hours, until it produced some effect. It soon removed the dropsical and asthmatic affections, and steel, with Seltzer water, restored him to health.

CASE XLVI.

August 6th. Mr. L——, Æt. 35. Ascites and anasarca. Pulv. Digital. grains three, repeated every fourth hour, until he had taken two scruples, removed every appearance of dropsy in a few days. He was then directed to take solution of merc. sublimat. and soon recovered his health and strength.

CASE XLVII.

August 16th. Mr. G——, of W——, Æt. 86. Asthma of many years duration, and lately an incipient anasarca, with a paucity of urine. He had never lived intemperately, was of a chearful disposition, and very sensible: for some years back had lost all relish for animal food, and his only support had been an ounce or two of bread and cheese, or a small slice of seed-cake, with three or four pints of mild ale, in the twenty-four hours. After trying chrystals of tartar, fixed alkaly, squills, &c. I directed three grains of Pulv. fol. Digital. made into pills, with G. ammoniac, to be given every six hours; this presently occasioned copious discharges of urine, removed his swellings, and restored him to his usual standard of health.

CASE XLVIII.

August 17th. T—— B——, Esq. of K——, Æt. 46. Jaundice, dropsy, and great hardness in the region of the liver. Infusion of Digitalis carried off all the effusion, and afterwards a course of deobstruent and tonic medicines removed his other complaints.

CASE XLIX.

August 23d. Mr. C——, Æt. 58. (The person mentioned at Case XXIII.) He had continued free from dropsy until within the last six weeks; his appetite was now totally gone, his strength extremely reduced, and the yellow of his jaundice changed to a blackish hue. The Digitalis was now tried in vain, and he died shortly afterwards.

CASE L.

August 24th. Mrs. W——, Æt. 39. Anasarcous legs and symptoms of hydrothorax, consequent to a tertian ague. Three grains of Pulv. Digitalis, given every fourth hour, occasioned a very copious flow of urine, and she got well without any other medicine.

CASE LI.

August 28th. Mr. J—— H——, Æt. 27. In consequence of very free living, had an ascites and swelled legs. I ordered him to take two grains of Fol. Digital. pulv. every two hours, until it produced some effect; a few doses caused a plentiful secretion of urine, but no sickness, or purging: in six days the swellings disappeared, and he has since remained in good health.

CASE LII.

September 27th. Mr. S——, Æt. 45. Had been long in an ill state of health, from what had been supposed an irregular gout, was greatly emaciated, had a sallow complexion, no appetite, costive bowels, quick and feeble pulse. The cause of his complaints was involved in obscurity; but I suspected the poison of lead, and was strengthened in this suspicion, upon finding his wife had likewise ill health, and, at times, severe attacks of colic; but the answers to my enquiries seemed to prove my suspicions fruitless, and, amongst other things, I was told the pump was of wood. He had lately suffered extremely from difficult breathing, which I thought owing to anasarcous lungs; there was also a slight degree of pale swelling in his legs. Pulv. fol. Digital. made into pills, with gum ammoniac and aromatic species, soon relieved his breathing. Attempts were then made to assist him in other respects, but with little good effect, and some months afterwards he died, with every appearance of a worn out constitution.

About two years after this gentleman's death, I was talking to a pump-maker, who, in the course of conversation, mentioned the corrosion of leaden pumps, by some of the water in this town, and instanced that at the house of Mr. S——, which he had replaced with a wooden one about three years before. The lead, he said, was eaten away, so as to be very thin in some places, and full of holes in others;—this accidental information explained the mystery.

The deleterious effects of lead seem to be considerably modified by the constitution of the patient; for in some families only one or two individuals shall suffer from it, whilst the rest receive it with impunity. In the spring of the year 1776, I was desired to visit Mrs. H——, of S—— Park, who had repeatedly been attacked with painful colics, and had suffered much from insuperable costiveness; I suspected lead to be the cause of her complaints, but was unable to trace by what means it was taken. She was relieved by the usual methods; but, a few months afterwards, I was desired to see her again: her sufferings were the same as before, and notwithstanding every precaution to guard against costiveness, she was never in perfect health, and seldom escaped severe attacks twice or thrice in a year; she had also frequent pains in her joints. I could not find any traces of similar complaints either in Mr. H——, the children, or the servants. Mrs. H—— was a water drinker, and seldom tasted any fermented liquor. The pump was of wood, as I had been informed upon my first visit. Her health continued nearly in the same state for two or three years more, but she always found herself better if she left her own house for any length of time. At length it occurred to me, that though the pump was a wooden one, the piston might work in lead. I therefore ordered the pump rods to be drawn up, and upon examination with a magnifying glass, found the leather of the piston covered with an infinite number of very minute shining particles of lead. Perhaps in this instance the metal was so minutely divided by abrasion, as to be mechanically suspended in the water. The lady was directed to drink the water of a spring, and never to swallow that from the pump. The event confirmed my suspicions, for she gradually recovered a good state of health, lost the obstinate costiveness, and has never to this day had any attack of the colic.

CASE LIII.

September 28th. Mrs. J——, Æt. 70. Ascites and very thick anasarcous legs and thighs, total loss of strength and appetite. Infusion of Digitalis was given, but, as had been prognosticated, with no good effect.

CASE LIV.

September 30th. Mr. A——, Æt. 57. A strong man; hydrothorax and swelled legs; in other respects not unhealthful. He was directed to take two grains of the Pulv. fol. Digit. made into a pill with gum ammoniac. Forty grains thus taken at intervals, effected a cure by increasing the quantity of urine, and he has had no relapse.

CASE LV.

November 2d. Mr. P—— of T——, Æt. 42. A very strong man, drank a great quantity of strong ale, and was much exposed to alterations of heat and cold. About the end of summer found himself short winded, and lost his appetite. The dyspnœa gradually increased, he got a most distressing sense of tightness across his stomach, his urine was little, and high coloured, and his legs began to swell; his pulse slender and feeble. From the 20th of September I frequently saw him, and observed a gradual and regular increase of all his complaints, notwithstanding the use of the most powerful medicines I could prescribe. He took chrystals of tartar, seneka, gum ammoniac, saline draughts, emetics, tinct. of cantharides, spirits of nitre dulcified, squills in all forms, volatile alkaly, calomel, Dover's powder, &c. Blisters and drastic purgatives were tried, interposing salt of steel and gentian. I had all along felt a reluctance to prescribe the Digitalis in this case, from a persuasion that it would not succeed. At length I was compelled to it, and directed one grain to be given every two hours until it should excite nausea. This it did; but, as I expected, it did no more. The reason of this belief will be mentioned hereafter. Five days after this last trial I gave him assafetida in large quantity, flattered by a hope that his extreme sufferings from the state of his respiration, might perhaps arise in part from spasm, but my hopes were in vain. I now thought of using an infusion of tobacco, and prescribed the following:

R. Fol. Nicotian. incis. ℨii.

Aq. bull. ℔ss.

Sp. Vini rectif. ℥i digere per horam.

I directed a spoonful of this to be given every two hours until it should vomit. This medicine had no better effect than the former ones, and he died some days afterwards.

CASE LVI.

November 6th. Mr. H——, Æt. 47. In the last stage of a phthisis pulmonalis, suffered much from dyspnœa, and anasarca. Squill medicines gave no relief. Digitalis in pills, with gum ammon. purged him, but opium being added, that effect ceased, and he continued to be relieved by them as long as he lived.

CASE LVII.

November 16th. Mrs. F——, Æt. 53. In August last was suddenly seized with epileptic fits, which continued to recur at uncertain intervals. Her belly had long been larger than natural, but without any perceptible fluctuation. Her legs and thighs swelled very considerably the beginning of this month, and now there was evidently water in the abdomen. The medicines hitherto in vain directed against the epileptic attacks, were now suspended, and two grains of the Pulv. fol. Digital. directed to be taken every six hours. The effects were most favourable, and the dropsical symptoms were soon removed by copious urinary discharges.

The attacks of epilepsy ceased soon afterwards. In February, 1781, there was some return of the swellings, which were soon removed, and she now enjoys very good health. Does not the narrative of this case throw light upon the nature of the epilepsy which sometimes attacks women, soon after the cessation of the menstrual flux?

1781.
CASE LVIII.

January 1st. Mrs. G——, of H——, Æt. 62. Ascites and very large hard legs. After trying various medicines, under the direction of a very able physician, I ordered her to take one grain of Pulv. Digital. every six hours, but it produced no effect. Other Medicines were then tried to as little purpose. About the end of February, I directed an infusion of the Fol. Digital. but with no better success. Other methods were thought of, but none proved efficacious, and she died a few weeks afterwards.

CASE LIX.

January 3d. Mrs. B——, Æt. 53. Ascites, anasarca, and jaundice. After a purge of calomel and jallap, was ordered the Infusion of Digitalis: it acted kindly as a diuretic, and greatly reduced her swellings. Other medicines were then administered, with a view to her other complaints, but to no purpose, and she died about a month afterwards.

CASE LX.

January 14th. Mr. B——, of D——. Jaundice and ascites, the consequences of great intemperance. Extremely emaciated; his tongue and fauces covered with apthous crusts, and his appetite gone. He first took tincture of cantharides with infusum amarum, then vitriolic salts, and various other medicines without relief; Infusum Digitalis was given afterwards, but was equally unsuccessful.

CASE LXI.

February 2d. I was desired by the late learned and ingenious Dr. Groome, to visit Miss S——, a young lady in the last state of emaciation from a dropsy. Every probable means to relieve her had been attempted by Dr. Groome, but to no purpose; and she had undergone the operation of the paracentesis repeatedly. The Doctor knew, he said, that I had cured many cases of dropsy, by the Digitalis, after other more usual methods had been attempted without success, and he wished this lady to try that medicine under my direction; after examining the patient, and enquiring into the history of the disease, I was satisfied that the dropsy was encysted, and that no medicine could avail. The Digitalis, however, was directed, and she took it, but without advantage. She had determined not to be tapped again, and neither persuasion, nor distress from the distension, could prevail upon her: I at length proposed to make an opening into the sac, by means of a caustic, which was done under the judicious management of Mr. Wainwright, surgeon, at Dudley. The water was evacuated without any accident, and the patient afterwards let it out herself from time to time as the pressure of it became troublesome, until she died at length perfectly exhausted.

Query. Is there not a probability that this method, assisted by bandage, might be used so as to effect a cure, in the earlier stages of ovarium dropsy?

CASE LXII.

February 27th. Mrs. O——, of T——, Æt. 52, with a constitution worn out by various complicated disorders, at length became dropsical. The Digitalis was given in small doses, in hopes of temporary benefit, and it did not fail to fulfil our expectations.

CASE LXIII.

March 16th. Mrs. P——, Æt. 47. Great debility, pale countenance, loss of appetite, legs swelled, urine in small quantity. A dram of Fol. siccat. Digital. in a half pint infusion was ordered, and an ounce of this infusion directed to be taken every morning. Myrrh and steel were given at intervals. Her urine soon increased, and the symptoms of dropsy disappeared.

CASE LXIV.

March 18th. Mr. W——, in the last stage of a pulmonary consumption became dropsical. The Digitalis was given, but without any good effect.

CASE LXV.

April 6th. Mr. B——, Æt. 63. For some years back had complained of being asthmatical, and was not without suspicion of diseased viscera. The last winter he had been mostly confined to his house; became dropsical, lost his appetite, and his skin and eyes turned yellow. By the use of medicines of the deobstruent class he became less discoloured, and the hardness about his stomach seemed to yield; but the ascites and anasarcous symptoms increased so as to oppress his breathing exceedingly. Alkaline salts, and other diuretics failing of their effects, I ordered him to take an infus. of Digitalis. It operated so powerfully that it became necessary to support him with cordials and blisters, but it freed him from the dropsy, and his breath became quite easy. He then took soap, rhubarb, tartar of vitriol, and steel, and gradually attained a good state of health, which he still continues to enjoy.

CASE LXVI.

April 8th. Mr. B——, Æt. 60. A corpulent man, with a stone in his bladder, from which at times his sufferings are extreme. He had been affected with what was supposed to be an asthma, for several years by fits, but through the last winter his breath had been much worse than usual; universal anasarca came on, and soon afterwards an ascites. Now his urine was small in quantity and much saturated, the dysuria was more dreadful than ever; his breath would not allow him to lie in bed, nor would the dysuria permit him to sleep; in this distressful situation, after having used other medicines to little purpose, I directed an infusion of Digitalis to be given. When the quantity of urine became more plentiful, the pain from his stone grew easier; in a few days the dropsy and asthma disappeared, and he soon regained his usual strength and health. Every year since, there has been a tendency to a return of these complaints, but he has recourse to the infusion, and immediately removes them.

CASE LXVII.

April 24th. Mr. M——, of C——, Æt. 57. Asthma, anasarca, jaundice, and great hardness and straitness across the region of the stomach. After a free exhibition of neutral draughts, alkaline salt, &c. the dropsy and difficult breathing remaining the same, he took Infusum Digitalis, which removed those complaints. He never lost the hardness about his stomach, but enjoyed very tolerable health for three years afterwards, without any return of the dropsy.

CASE LXVIII.

April 25th. Mrs. J——, Æt. 42. Phthisis pulmonalis and anasarcous legs and thighs. She took the Infusum Digitalis without effect. Myrrh and steel, with fixed alkaly, were then ordered, but to no purpose.

CASE LXIX.

May 1st. Master W——, of St——, Æt. 6. I found him with every symptom of hydrocephalus internus. As it was yet early in the disease, in consequence of ideas which will be mentioned hereafter, I directed six ounces of blood to be immediately taken from the arm; the temporal artery to be opened the succeeding day; the head to be shaven, and six pints of cold water to be poured upon it every fourth hour, and two scruples of strong mercurial ointment to be rubbed into the legs every day. Five days afterwards, finding the febrile symptoms very much abated, and judging the remaining disease to be the effect of effusion, I directed a scruple of Fol. Digital. siccat. to be infused in three ounces of water, and a table spoonful of the infusion to be given every third or fourth hour, until its action should be someway sensible. The effect was, an increased secretion of urine; and the patient soon recovered.

CASE LXX.

May 3d. Mrs. B——, Æt. 59. Ascites and anasarca, with strong symptoms of diseased viscera. Infusum Digitalis was at first prescribed, and presently removed the dropsy. She was then put upon saline draughts and calomel. After some time she became feverish: the fever proved intermittent, and was cured by the bark.

CASE LXXI.

May 3d. Mr. S——, Æt. 48. A strong man, who had lived intemperately. For some time past his breath had been very short, his legs swollen towards evening, and his urine small in quantity. Eight ounces of the Infus. Digitalis caused a considerable flow of urine; his complaints gradually vanished, and did not return.

CASE LXXII.

May 24th. Joseph B——, Æt. 50. Ascites, anasarca, and jaundice, from intemperate living. Infusion of Digitalis produced nausea, and lowered the frequency of the pulse; but had no other sensible effects. His disorder continued to increase, and killed him about two months afterwards.

CASE LXXIII.

June 29th. Mr. B——, Æt. 60. A hard drinker; afflicted with asthma, jaundice, and dropsy. His appetite gone; his water foul and in small quantity. Neutral saline mixture, chrystals of tartar, vinum chalybeat. and other medicines had been prescribed to little advantage. Infusion of Fol. Digitalis acted powerfully as a diuretic, and removed the most urgent of his complaints, viz. the dropsical and asthmatical symptoms.

The following winter his breathing grew bad again, his appetite totally failed, and he died, but without any return of the ascites.

CASE LXXIV.

June 29th. Mr. A——, Æt. 58. Kept a public house and drank very hard. He had symptoms of diseased viscera, jaundice, ascites, and anasarca. After taking various deobstruents and diuretics, to no purpose, he was ordered the Infusion of Digitalis: a few doses occasioned a plentiful flow of urine, relieved his breath, and reduced his swellings; but, on account of his great weakness, it was judged imprudent to urge the medicine to the entire evacuation of the water.

He was so much relieved as to be able to come down stairs and to walk about, but his want of appetite and jaundice continuing, and his debility increasing, he died in about two months.

CASE LXXV.

July 18th. Mrs. B——, Æt. 46. A little woman, and very much deformed. Asthmatical for many years. For several months past had been worse than usual; appetite totally gone, legs swollen, sense of great fulness about her stomach, countenance fallen, lips livid, could not lie down.

The usual modes of practice failing, the Digitalis was tried, but with no better success, and in about a month she died; not without suspicion of her death having been accelerated a few days, by her taking half a grain of opium. This may be a caution to young practitioners to be careful how they venture upon even small doses of opium in such constitutions, however much they may be urged by the patient to prescribe something that may procure a little rest and ease.

CASE LXXVI.

August 12th. Mr. L——, Æt. 65, the person whose Case is recorded at No. XXIV, had a return of his insanity, after near two years perfect health. He was extremely reduced when I saw him, and the medicine which cured him before was now administered without effect, for his weakness was such that I did not dare to urge it.

CASE LXXVII.

September 10th. Mr. V——, of S——, Æt. 47. A man of strong fibre, and the remains of a florid complexion. His disease an ascites and swelled legs, the consequence of a very free course of life; he had been once tapped, and taken much medicine before I saw him. The Digitalis was now directed: it lowered his pulse, but did not prove diuretic. He returned home, and soon after was tapped again, but survived the operation only a few hours.

CASE LXXVIII.

September 25th. Mr. O——, of M——, Æt. 63. Very painful and general swellings in all his limbs, which had confined him mostly to his bed since the preceding winter; the swellings were uniform, tense, and resisting, but the skin not discoloured. After trying guiacum and Dover's powder without advantage. I directed Infusion of Digitalis. It acted on the kidneys, but did net relieve him. It is not easy to say what the disease was, and the patient living at a distance, I never learnt the future progress or termination of it.

CASE LXXIX.

September 26th. Mr. D——, Æt. 42, a very sensible and judicious surgeon at B——, in Staffordshire, laboured under ascites and very large anasarcous legs, together with indubitable symptoms of diseased viscera. Having tried the usual diuretics to no purpose, I directed a scruple of Fol. Digital siccat. in a four ounce infusion, a table spoonful to be taken twice a day. The second bottle wholly removed his dropsy, which never returned.

CASE LXXX.

September 27th. Mrs. E——, Æt. 42. A fat sedentary woman; after a long illness, very indistinctly marked; had symptoms of enlarged liver and dropsy. In this case I was happy in the assistance of Dr. Ash. Digitalis was once exhibited in small doses, but to no better purpose than many other medicines. She suffered great pain in the abdomen for several weeks, and after her death, the liver, spleen, and kidneys were found of a pale colour, and very greatly enlarged, but the quantity of effused fluid in the cavity was not more than a pint.

CASE LXXXI.

October 28th. Mr. B——, Æt. 33. Had drank an immense quantity of mild ale, and was now become dropsical. He was a lusty man, of a pale complexion: his belly large, and his legs and thighs swollen to an enormous size. I directed the Infusion of Digitalis, which in ten days completely emptied him. He was then put upon the use of steel and bitters, and directed to live temperately, which I believe he did, for I saw him two years afterwards in perfect health.

CASE LXXXII.

November 14th. Mr. W——, of T——, Æt. 49. A lusty man, with an asthma and anasarca. He had taken several medicines by the direction of a very judicious apothecary, but not getting relief as he had been accustomed to do in former years, he came under my direction. For the space of a month I tried to relieve him by fixed alkaly, seneka, Dover's powder, gum ammoniac, squill, &c. but without effect. I then directed Infusion of Digitalis, which soon increased the flow of urine without exciting nausea, and in a few days removed all his complaints.

1782.
CASE LXXXIII.

January 23d. Mr. Q——, Æt. 74. A stone in his bladder for many years; dropsical for the last three months. Had taken at different times soap with squill and gum ammoniac; soap lees; chrystals of tartar, oil of juniper, seneka, jallap, &c. but the dropsical symptoms still increased, and the dysuria from the stone became very urgent. I now directed a dram of the Fol. Digit. siccat. in a half pint infusion, half an ounce to be given every six hours. This presently relieved the dysuria, and soon removed the dropsy, without any disturbance to his system.

CASE LXXXIV.

January 27th. Mr. D——, Æt. 86. The debility of age and dropsical legs had long oppressed him. A few weeks before his death his breathing became very short, he could not lie down in bed, and his urine was small in quantity. A wine glass of a weak Infusion of Digitalis, warmed with aromatics, was ordered to be taken twice a day. It afforded a temporary relief, but he did not long survive.

CASE LXXXV.

January 28th. Mr. D——, Æt. 35. A publican and a hard drinker. Ascites, anasarca, diseased viscera, and slight attacks of hæmoptoe. A dram of Fol. Digital. sicc. in a half pint infusion, of which one ounce was given night and morning, proved diuretic and removed his dropsy. He then took medicines calculated to relieve his other complaints. The dropsy did not return during my attendance upon him, which was three or four weeks. A quack then undertook to cure him with blue vitriol vomits, but as I am informed, he presently sunk under that rough treatment.

CASE LXXXVI.

January 29th. Mrs. O——, of D——, Æt. 53. A constant and distressing palpitation of her heart, with great debility. From a degree of anasarca in her legs I was led to suspect effusion in the Pericardium, and therefore directed Digitalis, but it produced no benefit. She then took various other medicines with the same want of success, and about ten months afterwards died suddenly.

CASE LXXXVII.

January 31st. Mr. T——, of A——, Æt. 81. Great difficulty of breathing, so that he had not lain in bed for the last six weeks, and some swelling in his legs. These complaints were subsequent to a very severe cold, and he had still a troublesome cough. He told me that at his age he did not look for a cure, but should be glad of relief, if it could be obtained without taking much medicine. I directed an Infusion of Digitalis, a dram to eight ounces, one spoonful to be taken every morning, and two at night. He only took this quantity; for in four days he could lie down, and soon afterwards quitted his chamber. In a month he had a return of his complaints, and was relieved as before.

CASE LXXXVIII.

January 31st. Mrs. J——, of S——, Æt. 67. A lusty woman, of a florid complexion, large belly, and very thick legs. She had been kept alive for some years by the discharge from ulcers in her legs; but the sores now put on a very disagreeable livid appearance, her belly grew still larger, her breath short, her pulse feeble, and she could not take nourishment. Several medicines having been given in vain, the Digitalis was tried, but with no better effect; and in about a month she died.

CASE LXXXIX.

February 2d. Mr. B——, Æt. 73. An universal dropsy. He took various medicines, and Digitalis in small doses, but without any good effect.

CASE XC.

February 24th. Master M——, of W——, Æt. 10. An epilepsy of some years continuance, which had never been interrupted by any of the various methods tried for his relief. The Digitalis was given for a few days, but as he lived at a distance, so that I could not attend to its effects, he only took one half pint infusion, which made no alteration in his complaint.

CASE XCI.

March 6th. Mr. H——, Æt. 62. A very hard drinker, and had twice had attacks of apoplexy. He had now an ascites, was anasarcous, and had every appearance of a diseased liver. Small doses of calomel, Dover's powder, infusum amarum, and sal sodæ palliated his symptoms for a while; these failing; blisters, squills, and cordials were given without effect. A weak Infusion of Digitalis, well aromatised, was then directed to be given in small doses. It rather seemed to check than to increase the secretion of urine, and soon produced sickness. Failing in its usual effect, the medicine was no longer continued; but every thing that was tried proved equally inefficacious, and he did not long survive.

CASE XCII.

May 10th. Mrs. P——, Æt. 40. Spasmodic asthma of many years continuance, which had frequently been relieved by ammoniacum, squills, &c. but these now failing in their wonted effects, an Infus. of Fol. Digitalis was tried, but it seemed rather to increase than relieve her symptoms.

CASE XCIII.

May 22d. Mr. O——, of B——, Æt. 61. A very large man, and a free liver; after an attack of hemiplegia early in the spring, from which he only partially recovered, became dropsical. The dropsy occupied both legs and thighs, and the arm of the affected side. I directed an Infusion of Digitalis in small doses, so as not to affect his stomach. The swellings gradually subsided, and in the course of the summer he recovered perfectly from the palsy.

CASE XCIV.

July 5th. Mr. C——, of W——, Æt. 28. Had drank very freely both of ale and spirits; and in consequence had an ascites, very large legs, and great fulness about the stomach. He was ordered to take the Infusion of Digitalis night and morning for a few days, and then to keep his bowels open with chrystals of tartar. The first half pint of infusion relieved him greatly; after an interval of a fortnight it was repeated, and he got well without any other medicine, only continuing the chrystals of tartar occasionally. I forgot to mention that this gentleman, before I saw him, had been for two months under the care of a very celebrated physician, by whose direction he had taken mercurials, bitters, squills, alkaline salts, and other things, but without much advantage.

CASE XCV.

March 6th. Mrs. W——, Æt. 36. In the last stage of a pulmonary consumption, took the Infus. Digitalis, but without any advantage.

CASE XCVI.

August 20th. Mr. P——, Æt. 43. In the year 1781 he had a severe peripneumony, from which he recovered with difficulty. At the date of this, when he first consulted me, the symptoms of hydrothorax were pretty obvious. I directed a purge, and then the Infusum Digitalis, three drams to half a pint, one ounce to be taken every four hours. It made him sick, and occasioned a copious discharge of urine. His complaints immediately vanished, and he remains in perfect health.

CASE XCVII.

September 24th. Mrs. R——, of B——, Æt. 35, the mother of many children. After her last lying in, three months ago, had that kind of swelling in one of her legs which is mentioned at No. VIII, XXVI, and XXXI. A considerable degree of swelling still remained; the limb was heavy to her feeling, and not devoid of pain. I directed a bolus of five grains of Pulv. Digitalis, and twenty-five of crude quicksilver rubbed down, with conserve of cynosbat. to be taken at bed-time, and afterwards an Infusion of red bark and Fol. Digitalis to be taken twice a day. There was half an ounce of bark and half a dram of the leaves in a pint infusion: the dose two ounces.

The leg soon began to mend, and two pints of the infusion finished the cure.

CASE XCVIII.

September 25th. Mr. R——, Æt. 60. Complained to me of a sickness after eating, and for some weeks past he had thrown up all his food, soon after he had swallowed it. He had taken various medicines, but found benefit from none, and had tried various kinds of diet. He was now very thin and weak; but had a good appetite. As several very probable methods had been prescribed, and as the usual symptoms of organic disease were absent, I determined to give him a spoonful of the Infusion of Digitalis twice a day; made by digesting two drams of the dried leaves in half a pint of cinnamon water. From the time he began to take this medicine he suffered no return of his complaint, and soon recovered his flesh and his strength.

It should be observed, that I had frequently seen the Digitalis remove sickness, though prescribed for very different complaints.

CASE XCIX.

September 30th. Mrs. A——, Æt. 38. Hydrothorax and anasarca. Her chest was very considerably deformed. One half pint of the Digitalis Infusion entirely cured her.

CASE C.

September 30th. Mr. R——, of W——, Æt. 47. Hydrothorax and anasarca. An Infusion of Digitalis was directed, and after the expected effects from that should take place, sixty drops of tincture of cantharides twice a day. As he was costive, pills of aloes and steel were ordered to be taken occasionally.

This plan succeeded perfectly. About a month afterwards he had some rheumatic affections, which were removed by guiacum.

CASE CI.

October 2d. Mrs. R——, Æt. 60. Diseased viscera; ascites and anasarca. Had taken various deobstruent and diuretic medicines to little purpose. The Digitalis brought on a nausea and languor, but had no effect on the kidneys.

CASE CII.

October 12th. Mr. R——, Æt. 41. A publican, and a hard drinker. His legs and belly greatly swollen; appetite gone, countenance yellow, breath very short, and cough troublesome. After a vomit I gave him calomel, saline draughts, steel and bitters, &c. He had taken the more usual diuretics before I saw him. As the dropsical symptoms increased, I changed his medicines for pills made of soap, containing two grains of Pulv. fol. Digital, in each dose, and, as he was costive, two grains of jallap. He took them twice a day, and in a week was free from every appearance of dropsy. The jaundice soon afterwards vanished, and tonics restored him to perfect health.

CASE CIII.

October 12th. Mr. B——, Æt. 39. Kept a public house, drank very freely, and became dropsical; he complained also of rheumatic pains. I directed Infusion of Digitalis, half an ounce twice a day. In eight days the swellings in his legs and the fulness about his stomach disappeared. His rheumatic affections were cured by the usual methods.

CASE CIV.

October 22d. Master B——, Æt. 3. Ascites and universal anasarca. Half a grain of Fol. Digital. siccat. given every six hours, produced no effect; probably the medicine was wasted in giving. An infusion of the dried leaf was then tried, a dram to four ounces, two tea spoonfuls for a dose; this soon increased the flow of urine to a very great degree, and he got perfectly well.

CASE CV.

October 30th. Mr. G——, of W——, Æt. 88. The gentleman mentioned in No. XLVII. His complaints and manner of living the same as there mentioned. I ordered an Infusion of the Digitalis, a dram and half to half a pint; one ounce to be taken twice a day; which cured him in a short time.

On March the 23d, 1784, he sent for me again. His complaints were the same, but he was much more feeble. On this account I directed a dram of the Fol. Digitalis to be infused for a night in four ounces of spirituous cinnamon water, a spoonful to be taken every night. This had not a sufficient effect; therefore, on the 22d of April, I ordered the infusion prescribed two years before, which soon removed his complaints.

He died soon afterwards, fairly worn out, in his ninetieth year.

CASE CVI.

November 2d. Mr. S——, of B——h——, Æt. 61. Hydrothorax and swelled legs. Squills were given for a week in very full doses, and other modes of relief attempted; but his breathing became so bad, his countenance so livid, his pulse so feeble, and his extremities so cold, that I was apprehensive upon my second visit that he had not twenty-four hours to live. In this situation I gave him the Infusum Digitalis stronger than usual, viz. two drams to eight ounces. Finding himself relieved by this, he continued to take it, contrary to the directions given, after the diuretic effects had appeared.

The sickness which followed was truly alarming; it continued at intervals for many days, his pulse sunk down to forty in a minute, every object appeared green to his eyes, and between the exertions of reaching he lay in a state approaching to syncope. The strongest cordials, volatiles, and repeated blisters barely supported him. At length, however, he did begin to emerge out of the extreme danger into which his folly had plunged him; and by generous living and tonics, in about two months he came to enjoy a perfect state of health.

CASE CVII.

November 19th. Master S——, Æt. 8. Ascites and anasarca. A dram of Fol. Digitalis in a six ounce infusion, given in doses of a spoonful, effected a perfect cure, without producing nausea.

1783.

The reader will perhaps remark, that from the middle of January to the first of May, not a single case occurs, and that the amount of cases is likewise less than in the preceding or ensuing years; to prevent erroneous conjectures or conclusions, it may be expedient to mention, that the ill state of my own health obliged me to retire from business for some time in the spring of the year, and that I did not perfectly recover until the following summer.

CASE CVIII.

January 15th. Mrs. G——, Æt. 57. A very fat woman; has been dropsical since November last; with symptoms of diseased viscera. Various remedies having been taken without effect, an Infusion of Digitalis was directed twice a day, with a view to palliate the more urgent symptoms. She took it four days without relief, and as her recovery seemed impossible it was urged no farther.

CASE CIX.

May 1st. Mrs. D——, Æt. 72. A thin woman, with very large anasarcous legs and thighs; no appetite and general debility. After a month's trial of cordials and diuretics of different kinds, the surgeon who had scarified her legs apprehended they would mortify; she had very great pain in them, they were very red and black by places, and extremely tense. It was evident that unless the tension could be removed, gangrene must soon ensue. I therefore gave her Infusum Digitalis, which increased the secretion of urine by the following evening, so that the great tension began to abate, and together with it the pain and inflammation. She was so feeble that I dared not to urge the medicine further, but she occasionally took it at intervals until the time of her death, which happened a few weeks afterwards.

CASE CX.

May 18th. I was desired to prescribe for Mary Bowen, a poor girl at Hagley. Her disease appeared to me to be an ovarium dropsy. In other respects she was in perfect health. I directed the Digitalis to be given, and gradually pushed so as to affect her very considerably. It was done; but the patient still carries her big belly, and is otherwise very well.

CASE CXI.

May 25th. Mr. G——, Æt. 28. In the last stage of a pulmonary consumption of the scrophulous kind, took an Infusion of Digitalis, but without any advantage.

CASE CXII.

May 31st. Mr. H——, Æt 27. In the last stage of a phthisis pulmonalis became dropsical. He took half a pint of the Infusum Digitalis in six days, but without any sensible effect.

CASE CXIII.

June 3d. Master B——, of D——, Æt. 6. With an universal anasarca, had an extremely troublesome cough. An opiate was given to quiet the cough at night, and 2 tea spoonfuls of Infus. Digit. were ordered every six hours. The dropsy was presently removed; but the cough continued, his flesh wasted, his strength failed, and some weeks afterwards he died tabid.

CASE CXIV.

June 19th. Mrs. L——, Æt. 28. A dropsy in the last stage of a phthisis. Infusum Digitalis was tried to no purpose.

CASE CXV.

June 20th. Mrs. H——, Æt. 46. A very fat, short woman; had suffered severely through the last winter and spring from what had been called asthma; but for some time past an universal anasarca prevailed, and she had not lain down for several weeks. After trying vitriolic acid, tincture of cantharides, squills, &c. without advantage, she took half a pint of Infus. Digitalis in three days. In a week afterwards the dropsical symptoms disappeared, her breath became easy, her appetite returned, and she recovered perfect health. The infusion neither occasioned sickness nor purging.

CASE CXVI.

June 24th. Mrs. B——, Æt. 40. A puerperal fever, and swelled legs and thighs. The fever not yielding to the usual practice, I directed an Infusion of Fol. Digitalis. It proved diuretic; the swellings subsided, but the fever continued, and a few days afterwards a diarrhœa coming on, she died.

CASE CXVII.

July 22d. Mr. F——, Æt. 48. A strong man, of a florid complexion, in consequence of intemperance became dropsical, with symptoms of diseased viscera, great dyspnœa, a very troublesome cough, and total loss of appetite. He took mild mercurials, pills of soap, rhubarb, and tartar of vitriol, with soluble tartar and dulcified spirits of nitre in barley water. After a reasonable trial of this plan, he took squill every six hours, and a solution of assafetida and gum ammoniac, to ease his breathing: finding no relief, I gave him chrystals of tartar with ginger; but his remaining health and strength daily declined, and he was not at all benefited by the medicines. I was averse to the use of Digitalis in this case, judging from what I had seen in similar instances of tense fibre, that it would not act as a diuretic. I therefore once more directed squill, with decoction of seneka and sal sodæ; but it was inefficacious. His strength being much broken down, I then ordered gum ammoniac, with small doses of opium, and infusum amarum, continuing the squill at intervals. At length I was urged to give the Digitalis, and considering the case as desperate, I agreed to do it. The event was as I expected; no increase in the urine took place; and the medicine being still continued, his pulse became slow, and he apparently sunk under its sedative effects. He was neither purged nor vomited; and had the Digitalis either been omitted altogether, or suspended upon its first effects upon the pulse being observed, he might perhaps have existed a week longer.

CASE CXVIII.

July 26th. Mr. W——, of W——, Æt. 47. Phthisis pulmonalis, jaundice, ascites, and swelled legs. As it was probable that the only relief I could give in a case so circumstanced, would be by carrying off the effused fluids. I tried squill and fixed alkaly; and these failing, I ordered the Infusum Digitalis. This had the desired effect, and, I believe, prolonged his life a few weeks.

CASE CXIX.

August 15th. Mrs. C——, Æt. 60. Ascites, anasarca, diseased viscera, paucity of urine, and total loss of appetite. These complaints had heretofore existed repeatedly, and had been removed by deobstruent and diuretic medicines; but in this attack the symptoms were suffered to exist a longer time and in a greater degree, before assistance was sought for. The remedies that used to relieve her were now exhibited to no purpose. Mild mercurials, soap, rhubarb, and squill were tried; but she grew rapidly worse. Saline draughts with acetum scilliticum seemed for a few days to check the progress of her complaint, but they soon lost their effect, and diarrhœa ensued upon every attempt to increase the frequency of the dose. Draughts with Infus. Digital. were then directed to be taken twice a day. The effect was a powerful action on the kidneys, and a reduction of the swellings, but without sickness. A degree of appetite returned, but still the tendency to diarrhœa existed, and kept her weak. Tonic medicines were then tried, but without advantage, and in a month it was necessary to have recourse to the Digitalis again. It was directed in a half pint mixture; an ounce to be taken thrice in twenty-four hours. On the 2d day, finding her symptoms very much relieved, she took in the absence of her nurse, nearly a double dose of the medicine. The consequence was great sickness, languor continuing for several days, and almost a total stop to the secretion of urine, from the time the sickness commenced.

The case now became totally unmanageable in my hands, and, after a fortnight, I was dismissed, and another physician called in; but she did not long survive.

This was not the first, nor the last instance, in which I have seen too large a dose of the medicine, defeat the very purpose for which it was directed.

CASE CXX.

August 22d. Mrs. S——, Æt. 36. Extreme faintiness; anasarcous legs and thighs; great difficulty of breathing, troublesome cough, frequent chilly fits succeeded by hot ones; night sweats, and a tendency to diarrhœa. Apprehensive that the more urgent symptoms were caused by water in the lungs, I directed an Infusion of Digitalis, with an ounce of diacodium to the half pint to prevent it purging, a wine glass full to be taken every night at bed-time, and a mixture with confect. cardiac. and pulv. ipecac. to be given in small doses after every loose stool.

On the fourth day she was better in all respects; had made a large quantity of water and did not purge. In a few days more she lost all her complaints, except the cough, which gradually left her, without any further assistance.

I was agreeably deceived in the event of this case, for I expected after the water was removed, to have had a phthisis to contend with.

CASE CXXI.

August 25th. T—— W——, Esq; Æt, 50. A free liver, diseased viscera, belly very tense, and much swollen; fluctuation perceptible, but the swelling circumscribed; pulse 132. This gentleman was under the care of my very worthy friend Dr. Ash, who, having tried various modes of cure to no purpose, asked me if I thought the Digitalis would answer in this case. I replied that it would not, for I had never seen it effectual where the swelling appeared very tense and circumscribed. It was tried however, but did not lessen the swelling. I mention this case, to introduce the above remark, and also to point out the great effect the Digitalis has upon the action of the heart; for the pulse came down to 96. He was afterwards tapped, and continued, for some time under our joint attendance, but the pulse never became quicker, nor did the swelling return.

CASE CXXII.

September 7th. Mr. L——, Æt. 43. After several severe attacks of ill formed gout, attended for some time past with jaundice and other symptoms of diseased viscera, the consequences of intemperate living, was sent to Buxton; from whence he returned in three weeks with ascites and anasarca. Under this complicated load of disease, I prescribed repeatedly without advantage, and at length gave him the Digitalis, which carried off the more obvious symptoms of dropsy; but the jaundice, loss of appetite, diseased viscera, &c. rendered his recovery impossible.

1784.
CASE CXXIII.

February 12th. Mrs. C——, Æt. 54. A strong short woman of a florid complexion; complained of great fullness across the region of the stomach; short breath, a troublesome cough, loss of appetite, paucity of urine; and had a brownish yellow tinge on her skin and in her eyes. She dated these complaints from a fall she had through a trap door about the beginning of winter. From the beginning of January to this time, she had been repeatedly let blood, had taken calomel purges with jallap; pills of soap, rhubarb and calomel; saline julep with acet. scillit. nitrous decoction, garlic, mercury rubbed down, infus. amarum purg. &c. After the failure of medicines so powerful, and seemingly so well adapted, and during the use of which all the symptoms continued to increase, it was evident that a favourable event could not be expected. However, I tried the infusum Digitalis, but it did nothing. I then gave her pills of quicksilver, soap and squill, with decoction of dandelion, and after some time, chrystals of tartar with ginger. Nothing succeeded to our wishes, and the increase of orthopnœa compelled me occasionally to relieve her by drastic purges, but these diminished her strength, more in proportion than they relieved her symptoms. Tincture of cantharides, sal diureticus and various other means were occasionally tried, but with very little effect, and she died towards the end of March.

CASE CXXIV.

March 31st. Miss W——, Æt. 60. Had been subject to peripneumonic affections in the winter. She had now total loss of appetite, very great debility, difficult breathing; much cough, a considerable degree of expectoration, and a paucity of urine. She had been blooded, taken soap, assaf. and squill, afterwards assaf. and ammon. with acet. scillit.: but all her complaints increasing, a blister was applied to her back, and the Digitalis infusion directed to be taken every night. The effect was an increased secretion of urine, a considerable relief to her breath, and some return of appetite; but soon afterwards she became hectic, spat purulent matter, and died in a few weeks.

CASE CXXV.

April 12th. Mrs. H——, of L——, Æt. 61. In December last this Lady, then upon a visit in London, was attacked with severe symptoms of peripneumony. She was treated as an asthmatic patient, but finding no relief, she made an effort to return to her home to die. In her way through this place, the latter end of December, I was desired to see her. By repeated bleedings, blisters, and other usual methods, she was so far relieved, that she wished to remain under my care. After a while she began to spit matter and became hectic. With great difficulty she was kept alive during the discharge of the abscess, and about the end of March she had swelled legs, and unequivocal symptoms of dropsy in the chest. Other diuretics failing, on the 12th of April I was induced to give her the Digitalis in small doses. The relief was great and effectual. After an interval of fifteen days, some swellings still remaining in the legs, I repeated the medicine, and with such good effect, that she lost all her complaints, got a keen appetite, recovered her strength, and about the end of May undertook a journey of fifty miles to her own home, where she still remains in perfect health.

CASE CXXVI.

April 17th. Mr. F——, Æt. 59. A very fat man, and a free liver; had long been subject to what was called asthma, particularly in the winter. For some weeks past his legs swelled, he had great sense of fullness across his stomach; a severe cough; total loss of appetite, thirst great, urine sparing, his breath so difficult that he had not lain down in bed for several nights. Calomel, gum ammoniac, tincture of cantharides, &c. having been given in vain, I ordered two grains of pulv. fol. Digitalis made into pills, with aromatic species and syrup, to be given every night. On the third day his urine was less turbid; on the fourth considerably increased in quantity, and in ten days more he was free from all complaints, and has since had no relapse.

CASE CXXVII.

May 7th. Miss K——, Æt. 8. After a long continued ague, became hectic and dropsical. Her belly was very large, and she had a total loss of appetite. Half a grain of fol. Digital, pulv. with 2 gr. of merc. alcalis. were ordered night and morning, and an infusion of bark and rhubarb with steel wine to be given in the day time. Her belly began to subside in a few days, and she was soon restored to health. Two other children in the family, affected nearly in the same way, had died, from the parents being persuaded that an ague in the spring was healthful and should not be stopped.—I know not how far the recovery in this case may be attributed to the Digitalis, but the child was so near dying that I dared not trust to any less efficacious diuretic.

CASE CXXVIII.

June 13th. Mr. C——, Æt. 45. A fat man, had formerly drank hard, but not latterly: last March began to complain of difficult breathing, swelled legs, full belly, but without fluctuation, great thirst, no appetite; urine thick and foul; complection brownish yellow. Mercurial medicines, diuretics of different kinds, and bitters, had been trying for the last three months, but with little advantage. I directed two grains of the fol. Digital. in powder to be taken every night, and infus. amar. with tinct. sacr. twice a day. In three days the quantity of his urine increased, in ten or twelve days all his symptoms disappeared, and he has had no relapse.

CASE CXXIX.

June 17th. Mr. N——, of W——, Æt. 54. A large man, of a pale complexion; had been subject to severe fits of asthma for some years, but now worse than usual. The intermitting pulse, the great disturbance from change of posture, and the swelled legs induced me to conclude that the exacerbation of his old complaint was occasioned by serous effusion. I directed pills with a grain and half of the pulv. Digital. to be taken every night, and as he was costive, jallap made a part of the composition. He was also directed to take mustardseed every morning and a solution of assafetida twice in the day. The effect of this plan was perfectly to our wishes, and in a short time he recovered his usual health. About half a year afterwards he died apoplectic.

CASE CXXX.

Mary B——. A young unmarried woman. Her disease appeared to me a dropsy of the right ovarium. She took an infusion of Digitalis, but, as I expected with no good effect. She is still, I am informed nearly in the same state.

CASE CXXXI.

July 12th. Mrs. A——, of C——, Æt. 56. After a series of indispositions for several years, became dropsical; and had long been confined to her chamber, unable to lie down or to walk. She was so feeble, her legs so much swelled, her breath so short, and the symptoms of diseased viscera so strong, that I dared not to entertain hopes of a cure; but wishing to relieve her more urgent symptoms, directed quicksilver rubbed down and fol. Digital. pulv. to be made into pills: the dose, containing two grains of the latter, to be given night and morning. She was also ordered to take a draught with a dram of æther twice a day, and to have scapulary issues. Her breath was so much relieved, that she was able soon afterwards to come down stairs; but her constitution was too much broken to admit of a recovery.

CASE CXXXII.

July 16th. Mr. B——, of W——, Æt. 31. After a tertian ague of 12 months continuation, suffered great indisposition for 10 months more. He chiefly complained of great straitness and pain in the hypochondriac region, very short breath, swelled legs, want of appetite. He had been under the care of some very sensible practitioners, but his complaints increased, and he determined to come to Birmingham. I found him supported upright in his chair, by pillows, every attempt to lean back or stoop forward giving him the sensation of instantaneous suffocation. He said he had not been in bed for many weeks. His countenance was sunk and pale; his lips livid; his belly, thighs and legs very greatly swollen; hands and feet cold, the nails almost black, pulse 160 tremulous beats in a minute, but the pulsation in the carolid arteries was such as to be visible to the eye, and to shake his head so that he could not hold it still. His thirst was very great, his urine small in quantity, and he was disposed to purge. I immediately ordered a spoonful of the infusum Digitalis every six hours, with a small quantity of laudanum, to prevent its running off by stool, and decoction of leontodon taraxacum to allay his thirst. The next day he began to make water freely, and could allow of being put into bed, but was raised high with pillows. Omit the infusion. That night he parted with six quarts of water, and the next night could lie down and slept comfortably. July 21st. he took a mild mercurial bolus. On the 25th. the diuretic effects of the Digitalis having nearly ceased, he was ordered to take three grains of the pulv. Digital. night and morning, for five days, and a draught with half an ounce of vin. chalyb. twice a day. August 15th. He took a purge of calomel and jallap, and some swelling still remaining in his legs, the Digitalis infusion was repeated. The water having been thus entirely evacuated, he was ordered saline draughts with acetum scilliticum and pills of salt of steel and extract of gentian. About a month after this, he returned home perfectly well.

CASE CXXXIII.

July 28th. Mr. A—— of W——, Æt. 29, became dropsical towards the close of a pulmonary consumption. He was ordered 12 grains of pulv. fol. cicutæ and 1 of Digitalis twice a day. No remarkable effect took place.

CASE CXXXIV.

July 31. Mr. M——, Æt 37. Hydrothorax. A single grain of fol. Digital. pulv. taken every night for three weeks cured him. The medicine never made him sick, but increased his urine, which became clear; whereas before it had been high coloured and turbid.

CASE CXXXV.

August 6th. Mr. C—— of B——, Æt. 42. Asthma and anasarca, the consequence of free living. He had been for some time under the care of an eminent physician of this place, but his complaints proving unusually obstinate, he consulted me. I directed an infusion of Digitalis to be taken every night, and a mixture with squill and tincture of cantharides twice every day. In about a week he became better, and continued daily mending. He has since enjoyed perfect health, having quitted a line of business which exposed him to drink too much.

CASE CXXXVI.

August 6th. Mr. M—— of C——, Æt. 44. Ascites and anasarca, preceded by symptoms of the epileptic kind. He was ordered to take two grains of pulv. Digitalis every morning, and three every night; likewise a saline draught with syrup of squills, every day at noon. His complaints soon yielded to this treatment, but in the month of November following he relapsed, and again asked my advice. The Digitalis alone was now prescribed, which proved as efficacious as in the first trial. He then took bitters twice a day, and vitriolic acid night and morning, and now enjoys good health.

Before the Digitalis was prescribed, he had taken jallap purges, soluble tartar, salt of steel, vitriol of copper, &c.

CASE CXXXVII.

August 10th. Mrs. W——, Æt. 55. An anasarcous leg, and sciatica; full habit. After bleeding and a purge, a blister was applied in the manner recommended by Cotunnius; and two grains of fol. Digital. with fifteen of fol. cicutæ were directed to be taken night and morning. The medicine acted only as a diuretic; the pain and swelling of the limb gradually abated; and I have not heard of any return.

I must here bear witness to the efficacy of Cotunnius's method of blistering in the sciatica, having used it in a great number of cases, and generally with success.

CASE CXXXVIII.

August 16th. Mrs. A—— of S——, Æt. 78. About the middle of Summer began to complain of short breath, great debility, and loss of appetite. At this time there were evident marks of effusion in the thorax, and some swelling in the legs. The advanced age, the weakness, and other circumstances of this patient, precluded every idea of her recovery; but something was to be attempted. Squills and other remedies had been tried; I therefore directed pills with two or three grains of the pulv. Digitalis to be taken every night for six nights, and a saline draught with forty drops of acetum scillit. twice in the day. She took but few of the draughts, seldom more than half one at a time, for they purged her, and she disliked them. The pills she took regularly, and with the happiest effect, for she could lie down, her breath was very much relieved, and a degree of appetite returned. Sept. 4th, some return of her symptoms demanded the further use of diuretics. I was afraid to push the Digitalis in so hazardous a subject, and therefore directed tinct. amara with tinct. canthar. and pills of squill, seneka, salt of tartar and gum ammoniac. These medicines did not at all check the progress of the disease, and on the 26th it became necessary to give the Digitalis again. The pills were therefore repeated as before, and infus. amarum with fixed alkaly ordered to be taken twice a day. The event was as favorable as before; and from this time she had no considerable return of dropsy, but languished under various nameless symptoms, until the middle or end of November.

CASE CXXXIX.

Aug. 16th. Mrs. P—— of S——, Æt. 50. For a particular account of this patient, see Mr. Yonge's second Case.

CASE CXL.

Sept. 20th. B—— B——, Esq. A true spasmodic asthma of many years continuance. After every method of relief had failed; both under my management, and also under the direction of several of the ablest physicians of this kingdom; I was induced to give him an infusion of the Digitalis. It was continued until nausea came on, but procured no relief.

CASE CXLI.

October 5th. Mr. R——, Æt. 43. (The patient mentioned at No. 102.) He had pursued his former mode of life, and had now a return of his complaints, with evident marks of diseased viscera. His belly not very large, but uncommonly tense. From this circumstance I did not expect the Digitalis to succeed, and therefore tried for some time to relieve him by the saline julep, with acet. scillitic. jallap, mercury, syrup of squill, with aq. cinnam. decoction of Dandelion, &c.; but these being administered without advantage, I was driven to the Digitalis. As he was very weak and much emaciated, I only gave two grains night and morning for five days. As no increase of urine took place, I used alkaline salt with tinct. cantharides:—This proving equally unsuccessful, on the 18th, I directed two ounces of the infusum Digitalis night and morning. This was continued until nausea took place, but the kidney secretion was not increased. Squill with opium, deobstruents of different kinds, sublimate solution, fixed alkaly, tobacco infusion, were now successively tried, but with the same want of success. The fullness of his belly made it necessary to tap him, and by repeating this operation he continued alive to the end of the year.

CASE CXLII.

October 19th. Mrs. R——, of B——, Æt. 47. Supposed Asthma, of eighteen months duration. She had kept her room for four months, and could not lie down without great disturbance; was very thin, and had totally lost all inclination for food. She was directed to take two gr. of pulv. fol. Digital. night and morning for five days, and infusum amarum, at the hours of eleven and five. In the course of a week she was much relieved, and could remain in bed all night. After a few days interval she took the Digitalis for five days more, and was soon after that well enough to come down stairs and conduct her family affairs.

In April 1785, she had a slight return, but not such as to confine her to her chamber. She experienced the same relief from the same medicine, but continuing it for seven days without interruption, it excited nausea.

CASE CXLIII.

October 28th. Mr. A——, subject to nephritis calculosa: After an attack of that kind, had still a troublesome sense of weight about his loins, now and then rising to pain, and a degree of dysuria, together with a want of appetite. These symptoms not readily yielding to the usual methods of treatment, I directed an infusion of Digitalis. The fourth dose caused a copious flow of urine; the sixth made him sick, and he was more or less sick at times for three days; but felt no more of his complaints.

I don't believe it is at all necessary to bring on sickness in these cases, but an unexpected absence from town prevented me from seeing him time enough to stop the exhibition of the medicine.

CASE CXLIV.

October 31st. Mrs. C——, of W——, Æt. 67. Asthma, and very thick hard legs of long continuance. The last month or two her breath worse than usual, her belly swollen, her thighs anasarcous, and her urine in small quantity. After trying garlic, squill, and purgatives without advantage, I directed the Digital. Infus. After taking about five ounces, her urine from thick and turbid, changed to clear and amber coloured, its quantity considerably increased, and her breathing easy. Contrary to my orders, but impelled by the relief she had found, she finished the remaining three ounces of the infusion, which made her very sick, and the free flow of urine immediately ceased. No medicine was administered for a fortnight, during which time her complaints increased. I then directed an infusion of tobacco, which affected her head, but did not increase her urine. She had recourse again to the Digitalis infusion, which once more removed the fulness of the belly, reduced the swellings of her thighs, and relieved her breath, but had no effect upon her legs.

CASE CXLV.

Nov. 2d. Miss B—— of C——, Æt. 22. A very evident fluctuation in the abdomen, which was considerably distended, whilst the rest of her frame was greatly emaciated. The presence of cough, hectic fever, and other circumstances, made it probable that this apparent ascites was caused by a purulent, and not a watery effusion. However it was possible I might be mistaken; the Digitalis was therefore given, but without any advantage.

The further progress of the disease confirmed my first opinion, and she died consumptive.

CASE CXLVI.

Nov. 4th. Mr. P—— of M——, Æt. 40. Subject to troublesome nephritic complaints, and after the last attack did not recover, or void the gravelly concretions as usual, a sense of weight across his loins continuing very troublesome. The usual medicines failing to relieve him, I ordered four grains of pulv. Digital. to be taken every other night for a week, and fifteen grains of mild fixed vegetable alkaly to be swallowed twice a day in barley water. He soon lost all his complaints; but we must not in this case too hastily attribute the cure to the Digitalis, as the alkaly has also been found a very useful medicine in similar disorders.

CASE CXLVII.

Nov. 4th. Mr. B—— of N——, Æt. 60. Had been much subject to gout, but his constitution being at length unable to form regular fits, he became dropsical. Pulv. fol. Digital. in doses of two or three grains, at bed-time, gave him some relief, but did not perfectly empty him. About three months afterwards he had occasion to take it again; but it then produced no effect, and he was so debilitated that it was not urged further.

CASE CXLVIII.

Nov. 8th. Mr. G——, Æt. 35. In the last stage of a phthisis pulmonalis, was attacked with a most urgent and painful difficulty of breathing. Suspecting this distress might arise from watery effusion in the chest, I gave him Digitalis, which relieved him considerably; and during the remainder of his life his breath never became so bad again.

CASE CXLIX.

Nov. 13th. Mrs. A—— of W——h——, Æt. 68. One of those rare cases in which no urine is secreted. It proved as refractory as usual to remedies, and not having ever succeeded in the cure of this disease, I determined to try the Digitalis. It was given in infusion, and, after a few doses, the secretion of a small quantity of urine seemed to justify the attempt. The next day, however, the secretion ceased, nor could it be excited again, tho' at last the medicine was pushed so as to occasion sickness, which continued at intervals for three days.

CASE CL.

Nov. 20th. Mrs. B——, Æt. 28. In the last stage of a pulmonary consumption became dropsical. I directed three grains of the pulv. Digital. to be taken daily, one in the morning, and two at night. She took twenty grains without any sensible effect.

CASE CLI.

Nov. 23d. Master W——, Æt. 7. Supposed hydrocephalus internus. A grain of pulv. fol. Digitalis was directed night and morning. After three days, no sensible effects taking place, it was omitted, and the mercurial plan of treatment adopted. The child lived near five months afterwards. Upon dissection near four ounces of water were found in the ventricles of the brain.

CASE CLII.

Nov. 26th. Mrs. W——, Æt. 65. I had attended this lady last winter in a very severe peripneumony, from which she narrowly escaped with her life. When the cold season advanced this winter, she perceived a difficulty in breathing, which gradually became more and more troublesome. I found her much harassed by a cough, which occasioned her to expectorate a little: the least motion increased her dyspnœa; she could not lie down in bed; her legs were considerably swelled, her urine small in quantity. I directed two grains of pulv. Digitalis made into a pill with gum ammoniac, to be taken every night, and to promote expectoration, a squill mixture twice in the day. Her urine in five days became clear and copious, and in a fortnight more she lost all her complaints, except a cough, for which she took the lac ammoniacum.

It is not improbable that the squill might have some share in this cure.

CASE CLIII.

December 7th. Mr. H——, Æt. 42. A large sat man, very subject to gravelly complaints. After an attack in the usual manner, continued to feel numbness in his lower limbs, and a sense of weight across his loins. I directed infusum Digitalis to be given every six hours. Six ounces made him sick, and he took no more. The next day his urine increased, a good deal of sand passed with it, and he lost his disagreeable feels, but the sickness did not entirely cease before the fourth day from its commencement.

CASE CLIV.

December 27th. Mr. B——, of H——, Æt. 55. Symptoms of hydrothorax, at first obscurely, afterwards more distinctly marked. Many things were tried, but the squill alone gave relief. At length this failed. About the third month of the disease, a grain of pulv. Digital. was ordered to be taken night and morning. This produced the happiest effects. In March following he had some slight symptoms of relapse, which were soon removed by the same medicine, and he now enjoys good health. For a more particular narrative see case the first, communicated by Mr. Yonge.

CASE CLV.

December 31st. Mrs. B——, of E——, Æt. 50. An ovarium dropsy of long continuance. She took three grains of pulv. Digital. every night at bed time, for a fortnight, but without any effect.

CASE CLVI.

A poor man in this town, after his kidneys had ceased to secrete urine for several days, was seized with hickup, fits of vomiting, and transient delirium. After examination I was satisfied the disease was the same as that mentioned at CXLIX. A very experienced apothecary having tried various methods to relieve him, I despaired of any success, but determined to try the Digitalis. It was accordingly given in infusion. At first it checked the vomitings, but did not occasion any secretion of urine.

1785.

The cases which have occurred to me in the course of this year, are numerous; but as the events of some of them are not yet sufficiently ascertained, I think it better to with-hold them at present.

FOOTNOTES:

Then resident at Lichfield, now at Derby.

This disease has lately been well described by Mr. White, of Manchester.

HOSPITAL CASES,
Under the Direction of the Author

The four following cases were drawn out at my request by Mr. Cha. Hinchley, late apothecary to the Birmingham Hospital. They are all the Hospital cases for which the Digitalis was prescribed by me, whilst he continued in that office.

CASE CLVII.

March 15th, 1780. John Butler, Æt. 30. Asthma and swelled legs. He was directed to take myrrh and steel every day, and three spoonfuls of infusum Digitalis every night. On the 8th of April he was discharged, cured of the swellings and something relieved of his asthmatic affections.

CASE CLVIII.

November 18th, 1780. Henry Warren, Æt. 60. This man had a general anasarca and ascites, and was moreover so asthmatic, that, neither being able to sit in a chair nor lie in bed, he was obliged constantly to walk about, or to lean forward against a window or table. You prescribed for him thus.

R. Aq. cinn. spt. ℥iv.

Oxymel. scillit.

Syr. scillit. aa. ℥i. m. cap. cochlear. larg. sexta quaque horâ.

This medicine producing no increased discharge of urine, on the 25th you ordered the infusion of Digitalis, two spoonfuls every four hours. After taking this for thirty six hours, his urine was discharged in very great quantity; his breath became easy, and the swellings disappeared in a few days, though he took no more of the medicine. On the 2d of December he was ordered myrrh and lac ammoniacum, which he continued until the 23d, when he was discharged cured, and is now in good health.

CASE CLIX.

November 3d, 1781. Mary Crockett, Æt. 40. Ascites and universal anasarca. For one week she took sal. diureticus and tincture of cantharides, but without advantage. On the 10th you directed the infusion of Digitalis, a dram and half to half a pint, an ounce to be taken every fourth hour. Before this quantity was quite finished, the urine began to be discharged very copiously. The medicine was then stopped as you had directed. On the 15th, being costive, she took a jallap purge, and on the 24th she was discharged cured.

CASE CLX.

March 16th, 1782. Mary Bird, Æt. 61. Great fullness about the stomach; diseased liver, and anasarcous legs and thighs. For the first week squill was tried in more forms than one, but without advantage. On the 22d she began with the Digitalis, which presently removed all the swelling.

She was then put upon the use of aperient medicines and tonics, and on the first of August was discharged perfectly cured.

The three following Cases were drawn up and communicated to me by Mr. Bayley, who succeeded Mr. Hinchley as apothecary to the Hospital at Birmingham:

Shiffnall, April 26th, 1785.

Dear Sir,

During my residence in the Birmingham General Hospital, I had frequent opportunities of seeing the great effects of the Digitalis in dropsy. As the exhibition of it was in the following instances immediately under your own direction, I have drawn them up for your inspection, previous to your publishing upon that excellent diuretic. Of its efficacy in dropsy I have considerable evidence in my possession, but consider myself not at liberty to send you any other cases except those you had yourself the conduct of. The Digitalis is a very valuable acquisition to medicine; and, I trust, it will cease to be dreaded when it is well understood.

I am, Sir, your obedient,
And very humble servant,
W. BAYLEY.

CASE CLXI.

Mary Hollis, aged 62, was admitted an out patient of the Birmingham General Hospital February 12th, 1784, labouring under all the effects of hydrothorax; her dread of suffocation during sleep was so great, that she always reposed in an elbow chair. She was directed to take two grains of Digitalis in powder every night and morning, and for a few days found great relief; but, on the eighth day, as she had complained of sickness, and had been considerably purged, she was ordered to desist taking any more of her powders. On the 14th day she was ordered an ounce of the following infusion twice in a day: R. Fol. Digital. purp. sicc. ℨiss. aq. bullient. ℔ss. digere per semi-horam, colaturæ adde tinct. aromatic ℨi. This infusion did not purge, but sometimes excited nausea, though not sufficient to prevent her from continuing its use. She grew gradually better, and on the 6th of May was discharged perfectly cured. The diuretic effects of the Digitalis were in this instance immediate.

CASE CLXII.

Edward James, Æt. 21. Admitted March 20th, 1784. Complained of great difficulty of breathing, pain in his head, and tightness about the stomach, with a trifling swelling of his legs. Ordered pil. scillit. ℈i. ter de die. On the third day his legs much more swelled, his breathing more difficult, and in every respect worse; his pulse very small and quick, complained when he turned in bed, of something like water rolling from one side of the thorax to the other. A remarkable blueness about the mouth and eyes, and purged considerably from the pil. scill. Ordered to omit the pills and to take ℨi. of infus. Digitalis every eight hours; the proportion ℨiss. to eight ounces of water and ℨi. of aq. n. m. sp.—7th Day, The infusion had neither purged, nor vomited him: he only complained once or twice of giddiness. His belly was now very hard, rather black on the right side the navel, and his legs amazingly swelled. Ordered a bolus with rhubarb and calomel, to be taken in the morning, and ℨii. julep salin. cum tinct. canthar. gutt. forty ter die.—12th Day, nearly in the same state, except his breathing which was somewhat more difficult, being now obliged to have his head considerably raised. Persistat—From this day to the 32d day he became hourly worse. His belly which at first was only hard, now evidently contained a large quantity of water, his legs were more swelled, and a large sphacelated sore appeared upon each outer ancle. Respiration was so much obstructed, that he was obliged to sit quite upright to prevent suffocation. He made very little water, not more than eight ounces in a day and a night, and was much emaciated. Ordered his purging bolus again, and ℨii. of a mixture with sal diuretic, ℨss. to ℨxii. three times in a day, and a poultice with ale grounds to his legs.

54th day. To this period there was not the least probability of his existing; his legs and thighs were one continued blubber, his thorax quite flat, and his belly so large that it measured within one inch as much as a woman's in this Hospital the day she was tapped, and from whom twenty seven pounds of coagulable lymph were taken. He made about three ounces of water in twenty-four hours: his penis and scrotum were astonishingly swelled, and no discharge from the sores upon his legs. Ordered to take a pill with two grains of powdered Foxglove night and morning. For a few days no sensible effect, but about the 60th day he complained of being continually giddy, and had some little pain in his stomach. He now made much more water, and dared to sleep. His appetite which through the whole of his illness had been very bad, was also better. 66th day. Breathing very much relieved, the quantity of water he made was three chamber pots full in a day and a night, each pot containing two quarts and four ounces, moderately full. Ordered to continue his pills, and his legs which were very flabby, to be rolled.

69th day. His belly nearly reduced to its natural size, still made a prodigious quantity of water, his appetite very good, habit of body rather lax, and his complexion ruddy. On the 2d of June, being still rather weak, he was ordered decoct. cort. ℨii. ter de die; and on the 12th was discharged from this Hospital perfectly cured.

W. BAYLEY.

Mr. Bayley's respectful compliments to Doctor Withering: he sends the case of Edward James, which he believes is pretty correct. He laments not having it in his power to send the measure of his belly, having unfortunately, mislaid the tape: he heard from James yesterday, and he is perfectly well.

General Hospital, August 5, 1784.

CASE CLXIII.

On the 26th February, 1785, Sarah Ford, aged 42, was admitted an out-patient of the Birmingham General Hospital: she complained of considerable pain in her chest, and great difficulty of breathing, her face was much swelled and her thighs and legs were anasarcous. She had extreme difficulty in making water, and with many painful efforts she did not void more than six ounces in twenty-four hours. She had been in this situation about six weeks, during which time she had taken ammoniacum, olibanum, and large quantities of squills, without any other effect than frequent sickness. Upon her commencing an Hospital patient, the following medicine was exhibited. R. gum ammoniac ℨii. pulv. fol. Digital. purp. ℈ii. sp. lavand. comp. ut fiat pil. 40. cap. ii. nocte maneque. She continued the use of these pills for a few days, without any sensible effect. On the eighth day her breathing was much relieved, her legs and thighs were not so much swelled, and in a day and a night she made five pints of water. By the 12th day her legs and thighs were nearly reduced to their natural size. She continued to make water in large quantities, and had lost her pain in the thorax. To the 20th of March, she made rapid advances towards health, when not a symptom of disease remaining, she was discharged.

COMMUNICATIONS FROM CORRESPONDENTS

London, Norfolk-street,
May 31st, 1785.

Sir,

I had the favour of your letter last week; and I shall be very happy if I can give you any intelligence relating to the Foxglove, that can answer the purpose in which you are so laudably engaged.

It is true that my brother, the late Dr. Cawley, was greatly relieved, and his life, perhaps, prolonged for a year, by a decoction of the Foxglove root; but why it had not a more lasting effect, it is necessary I should tell you that he had all the signs of a distempered viscera, long before any watery swellings appeared; it was manifest that his dropsy was merely symptomatic, and he could therefore only from time to time have any relief from medicine. In the year 1776, he returned from London to Oxon. having consulted several physicians at the former place, and Dr. Vivian at the latter, but without any success; and he was then told of a carpenter at Oxon. that had been cured of a Hydrops pectoris by the Foxglove root, and as he was a younger, and in other respects an healthy man, his cure, I believe, remains a perfect one.

I did not attend my brother whilst he took the medicine, and therefore I cannot speak precisely to the operation of it; but I remember, by his letters, that he was dreadfully sick and ill for several days before the secretion of urine came on, but which it did do to a great degree; relieved his breath, and greatly lessened the swelling in his legs and thighs; but the two instances I have lately seen in this part of the world, are much stronger proofs of the efficacy of it than my brother's case.

I am, &c.
ROBERT CAWLEY.

N. B. Whenever I have another opportunity of giving the Foxglove, it shall be in small doses:—In which I should hope it might succeed, although it might be more slowly. If you should try it with success, I should be glad to know what mode you made use of.

Dr. Cawley's prescription.

R. Rad. Digital. purpur. siccat. et contus. ℨii.

Coque ex aq. font. ℔ii. ad ℔i. colat. liquor. adde aq. junip. comp. ℨii.

Mell. anglic ʒi. m. sumat cochl. iv. omni nocte h. s. et mane.

—I have elsewhere remarked, that when the Digitalis has been properly given, and the diuretic effects produced, that an accidental over-dose bringing on sickness, has stopped the secretion of urine. In the present instance it likewise appears, that violent sickness may be excited, and continue for several days without being accompanied by a flow of urine; and it is probable that the latter circumstance did not take place, until the severity of the former abated. If Dr. Cawley had not had a constitution very retentive of life, I think he must have died from the enormous doses he took; and he probably would have died previous to the augmentation of the urinary discharge. For if the root from which his medicine was prepared, was gathered in its active state, he did not take at each dose less than twelve times the quantity a strong man ought to have taken. Shall we wonder then that patients refuse to repeat such a medicine, and that practitioners tremble to prescribe it? Were any of the active and powerful medicines in daily use to be given in doses twelve times greater than they are, and these doses to be repeated without attention to the effects, would not the patients die, and the medicines be condemned as dangerous and deleterious?—Yet such has been the fate of Foxglove!

A Letter to the Author, from Mr. Boden, Surgeon, at Broseley, in Shropshire.

Broseley, 25th May, 1785.

Dear Sir,

Have inclosed the prescriptions that contained the fol. Digital. which I gave to Thomas Cooke and Thomas Roberts.

Thomas Cooke, Æt. 49, had been ill about two or three weeks. When I saw him he had no appetite, and a constant thirst: a fullness and load in the stomach: the thighs, legs and hands, much swell'd, and the face and throat in a morning; was costive, and made but little water, which was high coloured; the pulse very weak, and his breath exceeding bad. June 17th. R. Argent, viv ʒi. cons. cynosbat. Ʒii. fol. Digital. pulv. gr. xv. f. pil. xxiv. capt. ii. omni nocte horâ decubitus. He was likewise purged by a bolus of argent. viv. jallap, Digit. elaterium and calomel, which was repeated on the fourth day, to the third time. From June 17th to the 29th, the symptoms were mostly removed, making water freely, and having plenty of stools; in a week after he was perfectly well, and remains so ever since. The cure was finished by steel and bitters.

Thomas Roberts, Æt. 40, had a deformed chest, was obliged to be almost in an erect posture when in bed; the other symptoms were nearly the same as Cooke's. August 3d. The pills prescribed June 17th for Cooke.—17th. A purging bolus of jalap and Digitalis, once a week. He continued the medicines till the latter end of August, when he got very well; but the complaint returned in Jan. worse than before. He is now much better, but I have great reason to believe the liver to be diseased.

I am, with the greatest respect,
Your very obliged humble servant,
DANIEL BODEN.

P. S. The second patient, on his relapse, took Digitalis again, combined with other things.

CASE communicated by Mr. Causer,
Surgeon, at Stourbridge, Worcestershire.

Mr. P—— of H—— M——, in the parish of Kingswinford, aged about 60; had been a strong healthy, robust, corpulent man; worked hard early in life at edge-tool making, and drank freely of strong malt liquor; for many years had been subject to gout in the extremities; for a few years past had been very asthmatic, and the gout in the extremities gradually decreased. When I first saw him, which was Sept. 12, 1779, his legs were anasarcous, his belly much swelled, and an evident fluctuation of water. His breathing very bad, an irregular pulse, and unable to lie down. His easiest posture was standing with his body leaning over a chair, in which situation he would continue many hours together, labouring for breath, with the sweat trickling down his face very profusely; the urine in very small quantity. Diuretics of every kind I could think of were used with very little or no advantage. Blisters applied to the legs relieved very considerably for a time, but by no means could I increase the urinary discharge. Warm stomachic medicines were given, and at the same time sinapisms applied to the feet, in hopes of enticing gout to the extremities, but without any good effect.—November 22d. The swelling considerably increasing, an emetic of acet. scillitic. was given, which acted very violently, and increased the urinary discharge considerably. He continued better and worse, using different kinds of diuretic and expectorating medicines until September 1781, when the disease was so much worse, I did not expect he could live many days. The acet. scillitic. was repeated, a table spoonful every half hour, till it acted briskly upwards and downwards; but without increasing the urinary discharge.—On the 17th of September I infused ʒiii. of the fol. Digitalis in ʒvi. of boiling water, for four hours; then strained it, and added ʒi. of tinct. aromatica.—On the 18th he began by taking one spoonful, which he was to repeat every half hour, till it made him very sick, unless giddiness, loss of sight, or any other disagreeable effect took place. I had never given the medicine before, and had prepared him to expect the operation to be very severe. I saw him again on the 21st; he had taken the medicine regularly, till the whole quantity was consumed, without perceiving the least effect of any kind from it, and continued well till the evening of the following day, when a little sickness took place, which increased, but never so as to occasion either vomiting or purging, but a surprising discharge of urine. The saliva increased so as to run out of his mouth, and a watery discharge from his eyes; these discharges continued, with a continual sickness, till the swelling was totally gone, which happened in three or four days. He afterwards took steel and bitters; and continued very comfortably, without any return of his dropsy, until the 7th of April 1782, when he was seized with an epidemic cough, which was very frequent with us at that time. His swellings now returned very rapidly, with the greatest difficulty in breathing, and he died in a few days. Blisters and expectorating medicines were used on this last return.

Extract of a Letter from Mr. Causer.

Mrs. S——, the subject of the following Case, was as ill as it is possible for woman to be and recover; from the inefficacy of the medicines used, I am convinced no medicine would have saved her but the Digitalis. I never saw so bad a case recovered; and it shews, that in the most reduced state of body, the medicine in small doses, will prove safe and efficacious.

N. B. The Digitalis, in pills, never occasioned the least sickness. She took two boxes of them.

CASE.

January 2d, 1785. Mrs. S——, of W——, near Kidderminster, aged 38, has been affected with dropsical swellings of her legs and thighs, about six weeks, which have gradually grown worse; has now great difficulty in breathing, which is much increased on moving; a very irregular, intermittent pulse, urine in very small quantity, and in the seventh month of her pregnancy: a woman of very delicate constitution, with tender lungs from her infancy and very subject to long continued coughs.

R. Pulv. scillæ gr. iii.

Jalap gr. x. syr. rosar. solut. tinct. senn. aa ʒii. aq. menth. v. simpl. ℥iss. m. mane sumend.

R. pulv. scillæ ℈i. G. ammoniac, sapon. venet. aa ʒiss. syr. q. s. f. pilul. 42 cap. iii. nocte maneque.

On the 7th found her worse, and the swelling increased; the urine about ℥x in the twenty-four hours.

R. Fol. siccat. Digital. ʒiii. coque in. aq. fontan. ℥xii. ad ℥vi. cola et adde. aq. juniper. comp. ℥ii. sacchar. alb. ℥ss. m. cap. cochlear. i. larg. 4tis horis.

She took about three parts of the medicine before any effect took place. The first was sickness, succeeded by a considerable discharge of urine. She continued the medicine till the whole was consumed, which caused a good deal of sickness for three or four days.

I saw her again on the 12th. The quantity of urine was much increased, and the swelling diminished. Pulse and breathing better.

R. Fol. sicc. Digital. G. assafetid. aa ʒi. calomel. pp. gr. x. sp. lavand. comp. q. s. fiat pilul. xxxii. cap. ii. omni nocte horâ somni.

A plentiful discharge of urine attended the use of these pills, and she got perfectly free from her dropsical complaints.

March 15th she was delivered: had a good labour, was treated as is usual, except in not having her breasts drawn, not intending see should suckle her child, being in so reduced a state. Continued going on well till the 18th, when she was seized with very violent pains across her loins, at times so violent as to make her cry out as much as labour pains. Enema cathartic. Fot. papav. applied to the part.

R. Pulv. ipecacoan. gr. vi. opii. gr. iv. syr. q. s. fiat pilul. vi. capt. i. 2da quaque horâ durante dolore.

R. Julep, e camphor, sp. minder. aa ʒii. capt. cochlear, i. larg. post singul. pilul.

19th. Breathing short, unable to lie down, very irregular low pulse scarcely to be felt, fainty, and a universal cold sweat: no appetite nor thirst, spasmodic pains at times across the loins very violent, but not so frequent as on the preceding day.

R. Gum ammoniac, assafetid. aa ʒi. camphor. gr. xii. fiat pilul. 24. capt. ii. 3tia quaque horâ in cochlear. ii. mixtur. seq.

R. Balsam. peruv. ʒiii. mucilag. G. arab. q. s. flor. zinci g. vi. aq. menth. simp. ℔ss. m.

Applic. Emp. vesicat. femorib. internis.

R. Sp. vol. fœtid. elixir. paregor. balsam.
Traumatic. aa ʒiii. capt. cochlear. parv. urgente languore.

20th. Much the same; makes very little water, and the legs begin to swell.—Applic. Emp. e pice burgund. lumbis.

23d. The swelling very much increased.—Capt. gutt. xv. acet. scillitic. ter die in two spoonfuls of the following mixture.

R. Infus. baccar. juniper, ʒvi. tinct. amar. tinct. stomachic. aa ʒi. m.

25th. Much the same.

28th. The swelling considerably increased, in other respects very much the same.

30th. Breathing very bad, with cough and pain across the sternum, unable to lie down, legs, thighs, and body very much swelled, urine not more than four or five ounces in the twenty-four hours; hot and feverish, with thirst.

Applic. Emp. vesicat. stomacho et sterno.

R. G. assafetid. ℈ii. pulv. jacob. ℈i. rad. scill. recent. gr. xii. extract. thebaic. gr. iv. f. pilul. xvi. cap. iv. omni nocte.

R. Sal. nitr. sal. diuretic. aa ʒii. pulv. e contrayerv. comp. ʒi. sacchar. ʒi. emuls. commun. ℔i. aq. cinnam. simpl. ʒi. m. capt. cochlear. iv. ter die.

April 2d. Much the same, no increase of urine.

3d. Breathing much relieved by the blister, which runs profusely. Repeated the medicines, and continued them till the

12th. The cough very bad, pulse irregular, swelling much increased, urine in very small quantity, not at all increased; great lowness and fainting. She desired to have some of the pills which relieved her so much when with child. I was almost afraid to give them, but the inefficacy of the other medicines gave me no hopes of a cure from continuing them, which made me venture to comply with her request.

R. Fol. siccat. Digital. G. assafetid. aa ʒi. sp. lavand. comp. q. s. f. pilul. xxxii. cap. ii. omni mane; et omni node cap. pilul. e styrace gr. vi.

17th. Considerable increase of urine.

21st. Swelling a good deal diminished; urine near four pints in twenty-four hours, which is more than double the quantity she drinks.

Applic. Emp. vesicat. femoribus internis.

The Digitalis pills and opiate at bed-time continued. Takes a tea cup of cold chamomile tea every morning.

25th. Swelling much diminished, makes plenty of water, appetite much mended, cough and breathing better. She omitted the medicine for three days; the urine began to diminish, the swelling and shortness of breathing worse. On repeating it for two days, the discharge was again augmented, and a diminution of the swelling succeeded. She has continued the pills ever since till the 14th of May; the dropsical symptoms and cough are entirely gone, the water is in sufficient quantity, her strength is recovered, and she has a good appetite. All she now complains of is a weight across her stomach, which is worse at times, and she thinks, unless it can be removed, she shall have a return of her dropsy.

Extract of a Letter from Doctor Fowler, Physician, at Stafford.

I understand you are going to publish on the Digitalis, which I am glad to hear, for I have long wished to see your ideas in print about it, and I know of no one (from the great attention you have paid to the subject) qualified to treat on it but yourself. There are gentlemen of the faculty who give verbal directions to poor patients, for the preparing and taking of an infusion or decoction of the green plant. Would one suppose that such gentlemen had ever attended to the nature and operation of a sedative power on the functions, particularly the vital? Is not such a vague and unscientific mode of proceeding putting a two edged sword into the the hands of the ignorant, and the most likely method to damn the reputation of any very active and powerful medicine? And is it not more than probable that the neglect of adhereing to a certain and regular preparation of the nicotiana, and the want (of what you emphatically call) a practicable dose, have been the chief causes of the once rising reputation of that noted plant being damned above a century ago? In short, the Digitalis is beginning to be used in dropsies, (although some patients are said to go off suddenly under its administration) somewhat in the style of broom ashes; and, in my humble opinion, the public, at this very instant, stand in great need of your precepts, guards, and cautions towards the safe and successful use of such a powerful sedative diuretic; and I have no doubt of your minute attention to those particulars, from a regard to the good and welfare of mankind, as well as to your own reputation with respect to that medicine.

I remember an officer in the Staffordshire militia, who died here of a dropsy five years ago. The Digitalis relieved him a number of times in a wonderful manner, so that in all probability he might have obtained a radical cure, if he would have refrained from hard drinking. I understood it was first ordered for him by a medical gentleman, and its sedative effects proved so mild, and diuretic operation so powerful, that he used to prepare it afterwards for himself, and would take it with as little ceremony as he would his tea. It is said, that he was so certain of its successful operation, that he would boast to his bacchanalian companions, when much swelled, you shall see me in two days time quite another man.

CASES communicated by Mr. J. Freer, jun. Surgeon, in Birmingham.

CASE I.

Nov. 1780. Mary Terry, aged 60. Had been subject to asthma for several years; after a severe fit of it her legs began to swell, and the quantity of urine to diminish. In six weeks she was much troubled with the swellings in her thighs and abdomen, which decreased very little when she lay down: she made not quite a pint of water in the twenty-four hours. I ordered her to take two spoonfuls of the infusion of Foxglove every three hours. By the time she had taken eight doses her urine had increased to the quantity of two quarts in the day and night, but as she complained of nausea, and had once vomited, I ordered the use of the medicine to be suspended for two days. The nausea being then removed, she again had recourse to it, but at intervals of six hours. The urine continued to discharge freely, and in three weeks she was perfectly cured of her swellings.

CASE II.

December, 1782. A poor woman, who had been afflicted with an ague during the whole of her pregnancy, and for two months with dropsical swellings of the feet, legs, thighs, abdomen, and labia pudenda; was at the expiration of the seventh month taken in labour. On the day after her delivery the ague returned, with so much violence as to endanger her life. As soon as the fit left her, I began to give her the red bark in substance, which had the desired effect of preventing another paroxysm. She continued to recover her health for a fortnight, but did not find any diminution in the swellings; her legs were now so large as to oblige her to keep constantly on the bed, and she made very little water. I ordered her the infusion of Foxglove three times a day, which, on the third day, produced a very copious discharge of urine, without any sickness; she continued the use of it for ten days, and was then able to walk. Having lost all her swellings, and no complaint remaining but weakness, the bark and steel compleated the cure.

Extract of a Letter from Doctor Jones, Physician, in Lichfield.

Anxious to procure authentic accounts from the patients, to whom I gave the Foxglove, I have unavoidably been delayed in answering your last favour. However, I hope the delay will be made up by the efficacy of the plant being confirmed by the enquiry. Long cases are tedious, and seldom read, and as seldom is it necessary to describe every symptom; for every case would be a history of dropsy. I shall therefore content myself with specifying the nature of the disease, and when the dropsy is attended with any other affection shall notice it.

Two years have scarcely elapsed since I first employed the Digitalis; and the success I have had has induced me to use it largely and frequently.

CASE I.

Ann Willott, 50 years of age, became a patient of the Dispensary on the 11th of April 1783. She then complained of an enlargement of the abdomen, difficulty of breathing, particularly when lying, and costiveness. She passed small quantities of high-coloured urine; and had an evident fluctuation in the belly. Her legs were œdematous. Chrystals of tartar, squills, &c. had no effect. The 13th of June she took two spoonfuls of a decoction of Foxglove, containing three drams of the dry leaves, in eight ounces, three times a day. Her urine soon increased, and in a few days she passed it freely, which continued, and her breath returned.

CASE II.

Mr. ——, 45 years of age, had been long subject to dropsical swellings of the legs, and made little water. Two spoonfuls of the same decoction twice a day, soon relieved him.

CASE III.

Mrs. ——, aged 70 years. A lady frequently afflicted with the gout, and an asthmatical cough. After a long continuance of the latter, she had a great diminution of urine, and considerable difficulty of breathing, particularly on motion, or when lying. Her body was much bound. There was, however, no apparent swelling. She took three spoonfuls of an aperient decoction of forty-five grains in six ounces and a half, every other morning. The urine was plentiful those days, and her breathing much relieved. In two or three weeks after the use of it she was perfectly restored. The purgative medicine neither increased the urine, nor relieved the breathing, till the Foxglove was added.

This spring she long laboured with the gout in her stomach, which terminated in a fit in her hand. During the whole of this tedious illness, of nearly three months, she passed little urine, and her breathing was again short.

She took the same preparation of Foxglove without any diuretic effect, and afterwards two and three grains of the powder twice a day with as little. The dulcified spirits of vitriol, however, quickly promoted the urinary secretion.

CASE IV.

Mr. C——, 46 years of age, had dropsical swellings of the legs, and passed little urine. He took the decoction with three drams, and was soon relieved.

CASE V.

Lady——, took three grains of the dried leaves twice a day, for swelled legs, and scantiness of urine, without effect.

CASE VI.

Mrs. Slater, aged 36 years. For dropsy of the belly and legs, and scantiness of urine, of several weeks standing, took three grains of the powder twice a day, and was quite restored in ten days. She took many medicines without effect.

CASE VII.

Mrs. P——, in her 70th year, took three grains of the powder twice a day, for scantiness of urine, and swelled legs, without effect.

CASE VIII.

Ann Winterleg, in her 26th year, had dropsical swellings of the legs, and passed little urine: she was relieved by two drams, in an eight ounce decoction.

CASE IX.

William Brown, aged 76. In the last stage of dropsy of the belly and legs, found a considerable increase of his urine by a decoction of Foxglove, but it was not permanent.

CASE X.

Mr. ——, — years of age, and of very gross habit of body, became highly dropsical, and took various medicines, without effect. One ounce of the decoction, with three drams of the dry leaves in eight ounces, twice or three times a day, increased his urine prodigiously. He was evidently better, but a little attendant nausea overcame his resolution, and in the course of some weeks afterwards he fell a victim to his obstinacy.

CASE XI.

Mrs. Smith, about 50 years of age, after a tedious illness of many weeks, had a jaundice, and became dropsical in the legs. Two spoonfuls of the decoction, with three drams twice a day, increased her urine, and abated the swelling.

CASE XII.

Widow Chatterton, about 60 years of age. Took the decoction in the same way for dropsy of the legs, with little effect.

CASE XIII.

—— Genders, about thirty-four years of age, was delivered of three children, and became dropsical of the abdomen. She passed little or no urine, had constant thirst, and no appetite. She took two spoonfuls of an eight ounce decoction, with three drams twice a day. By the time she had finished the bottle, (which must have been on the fourth day,) she had evacuated all her water, and could go about. Her appetite increased with every dose, and she recovered without farther help.

CASE XIV.

Miss M—— M——, in her 20th year. Had been infirm from her cradle, and, after various sufferings, had an astonishing œdematous swelling of one leg and thigh, of many weeks standing. She passed little or no urine, and had all her other complaints. She took 2 spoonfuls of an eight oz. decoction of two drams, twice a day. Her urine immediately increased; and, on the third day, the swelling had entirely subsided.

CASE XV.

Mr. P——, 65 years of age, and of a full habit of body. Had lived freely in his youth, and for many years led rather an inactive life. His health was much impaired several months, and he had a considerable distention, and evident fluctuation in the abdomen, and a very great œdema of the legs and thighs. His breathing was very short, and rather laborious, appetite bad, and thirst considerable. His belly was bound, and he passed very small quantities of high-coloured urine, that deposited a reddish matter. He had taken medicines some time, and, I believe, the Digitalis; and had been better.

A blister was applied to the upper and inside of each thigh; he took two spoonfuls of the decoction, with three drams of the dry leaves, two or three times a day; and some opening physic occasionally.

He lived at a considerable distance, and I did not visit him a second time; but I was well informed, about ten days or a fortnight afterwards, that his urine increased amazingly upon taking the decoction, and that the water was entirely evacuated.

CASE XVI.

Mrs. G——, aged 50 years. After being long ailing, had a large collection of water in the abdomen and lower extremities. Her urine was high-coloured, in small quantities, and had a reddish sediment. She took the decoction of Digitalis, squills, &c. without any effect. The chrystals of tartar, however, cured her speedily.

CASE XVII.

Mr. ——, about 50 years of age, complained of great tension and pain across the abdomen, and of loss of appetite; his urine, he thought, was less than usual, but the difference was so trifling he could speak with no certainty: his belly seemed to fluctuate. Among other things he tried the Foxglove leaves dried, twice a day; and, although it appeared to afford him relief, yet the effect was not permanent.

CASE XVIII.

Mr. W——, aged between 60 and 70 years; and rather corpulent: was considerably dropsical, both of the belly and legs, and his urine in small quantities. Three grains of the dry leaves, twice a day, evacuated the water in less than a fortnight.

CASE XIX.

Sarah Taylor, 40 years of age, was admitted into the Dispensary for dropsy of the abdomen and legs; and was relieved by the Decoctum digitalianum.

CASE XX.

Lydia Smith, aged 60. Dispensary. Laboured many years under an asthma, and became dropsical. She took the decoction without effect.

CASE XXI.

John Leadbeater, aged 15 years. Had a quotidian intermittent, which was removed by the humane assistance of an amiable young lady. His intermittent was soon attended by a very considerable ascites; for which he became a patient of the Dispensary. He took a decoction of Foxglove night and morning. His urine increased immediately, and he lost all his complaints in four days.

CASE XXII.

William Millar, aged 50 years. Admitted into the Dispensary for a tertian ague, and general dropsy. The dropsy continuing after the ague was removed, and his urine being still passed in small quantities; he took the powdered leaves, and recovered his health in five days.

CASE XXIII.

Ann Wakelin, 10 years of age. Had for several weeks a dropsy of the belly after an ague. She took a decoction of Foxglove, which removed all complaint by the fourth day.

CASE XXIV.

Ann Meachime; a Dispensary patient. Had an ascites and scantiness of urine. She took the powder of Foxglove, and evacuated all her water in three days.

It may not be improper to observe, 1st. That various diuretics had long been given in many of these cases before I was consulted. And, 2dly. That the exhibition of the Foxglove was but seldom attended with sickness.

REMARKS.

These Cases, thus liberally communicated by my friend, Dr. Jones, are more acceptable, as they seem to contain a faithful abstract from his notes, both of the unsuccessful as well as the successful Cases.

The following Tabular View of them will give us some Idea of the efficacy of the Medicine.

Anasarca	7 Cases	Cured	3
		Relieved	1
		Failed	3
Ascites	5 Cases	Cured	4
		Relieved	1
Œdematous leg	1 Case	Cured	1

Ascites and anasarca	7 Cases	Cured	4
		Relieved	2
		Failed	1
Asthma and dropsy	1 Case	Failed	1
Hydrothorax and gout	1 Case	Cured	1
- - - - -, ascites and anasarca	2 Cases	Cured	2

A CASE of Anasarca communicated by Mr. Jones, Surgeon, in Birmingham.

Dear Sir,

Having lately experienced the diuretic powers of the Foxglove, in a case of anasarca; I do myself the pleasure of communicating a short history of the treatment to you.

I am, &c.
W. JONES.

Birmingham,
May 17th, 1785.

My patient, Mrs. C——, who is in her 51st year, had the following symptoms, viz. alternate swelling of the legs and abdomen, a little cough, shortness of breath in a morning, thirst, weak pulse, and her urine, which was so small in quantity as seldom to amount to half a pint in twenty-four hours, deposited a clay-coloured sediment.

April 16th, 1785, I directed the following form:

R. Fol. Digitalis siccat. ʒii.
Aq. fontanæ bullient. ℥viii. f. infus. et cola. Sumat cochl. larga iii. o. n. et mane.

On the 17th she had taken twice of the infusion, and though by mistake only two tea spoonfuls for a dose, yet the quantity of urine was increased to about a pint in the twenty-four hours. She was then directed to take two table spoonfuls night and morning. And.

On the 18th, a degree of nausea was produced. A pint and half of urine was made in the last twenty-four hours. During the time above specified she had two or three stools every day. The infusion was now omitted.

On the 19th the swelling of the legs was removed. A degree of nausea took place in the morning, and increased so much during the day, that she vomited up all her food and medicine. As she was very low, and complained of want of appetite, a cordial julep was directed to be taken occasionally, as well as red port and water, mint tea, &c. She informed me that whatever she took generally staid about an hour before it came up again, and that the mint tea staid longest on the stomach. The vomiting decreased gradually, and ceased on the 22d. The discharge of urine remained considerable during the three following days, but its quantity was not measured.

22d. A dose of neutral saline julep was directed to be taken every fourth hour.

On the 23d she complained of thirst, and thought the discharge of urine not so copious as on the preceding days, therefore the saline julep was continued every fourth hour, with the addition of thirty drops of the following medicine:

R. Aceti scillitic. ʒvi.
Tinct. aromat. ʒii.
Tinct. thebaic. gutt. xx. m.

The bowels have been kept open from the 19th, by the occasional use of emollient injections.

On the 24th the legs were much swelled again; she complained of languor and a degree of nausea. The discharge of urine increased a little since the 23d. Her pulse was low and her tongue white. The urine, which had been rendered clear by the infusion of Foxglove, now deposited a whitish sediment.

On the 25th her appetite began to return, the swelling of the legs diminished, and she thought herself much relieved. The urine was considerable in quantity, and clear.

On the 26th she was thirsty and languid. The swelling was removed; the quantity of urine discharged in the last twenty-four hours was about a pint. She continued to mend from this time, and is now in good health.

A giddiness of the head, more or less remarkable at times, was observed to follow the use of the Foxglove, and it lasted nine or ten days.

This is the second time that I have relieved this patient by the infusion of Foxglove. I used the same proportion of the fresh leaves the first time as I did of the dried ones the last. The violent vomiting which followed the use of the infusion made with the dried leaves, did not take place with the fresh though she took near a pint made with the same proportion of the herb fresh gathered.

REMARKS.

The above is a very instructive case, as it teaches us how small a quantity of the infusion was necessary to effect every desirable purpose. At first sight it may appear from the concluding paragraph, that the green leaves ought to be preferred to the dried ones, as being so much milder in their operation; but let it be noticed, that the same quantity of infusion was prepared from the same weight of the green as of the dried leaves, and consequently, as will appear hereafter, the infusion with the dried leaves was five times the strength of that before prepared from the green ones. We need not wonder, therefore, that the effects of the former were so disagreeable, when the dose was five times greater than it ought to have been. But what makes this matter still more obvious, is the mistake mentioned at first, of two tea spoonfuls only being given for a dose. Now a tea spoonful, containing about a fourth or a fifth part of the contents of a table spoon, the dose then given, was very nearly the same as that which had before been taken of the infusion of the green leaves, and it produced precisely the same effects for it increased the urinary discharge, without exciting the violent vomiting.

Letter from Doctor Johnstone, Physician, in Birmingham.

Dear Sir,

The following cases are selected from many others in which I have given the Digitalis purpurea; and from repeated experience of its efficacy after other diuretics have failed. I can recommend it as an effectual, and when properly managed, a safe medicine.

I am, &c.
E. JOHNSTONE.

Birmingham, May 26, 1785.

March 8th, 1783, I was called to attend Mr. G——, a gentleman of a robust habit, who had led a regular and temperate life, Æt. 68. He was affected with great difficulty of respiration, and cough particularly troublesome on attempting to lie down, œdematous swellings of the legs and thighs, abdomen tense and sore on being pressed, pain striking from the pit of the stomach to the back and shoulders; almost constant nausea, especially after taking food, which he frequently threw up; water thick and high-coloured, passed with difficulty and in small quantity; body costive; pulse natural; face much emaciated, eyes yellow and depressed. He had been subject to cough and difficulty of breathing in the winter for several years; and about four years before this time, after being exposed to cold, was suddenly deprived of his speech and the use of the right side, which he recovered as the warm weather came on; but since that time had been remarkably costive, and was in every respect much debilitated. He first perceived his legs swell about a year ago; by the use of medicines and exercise, the swellings subsided during the summer, but returned on the approach of winter, and gradually increased to the state in which I found them, notwithstanding he had used different preparations of squills and a great variety of other diuretic medicines. I ordered the following mixture.

R. Foliorum Digitalis purpur. recent. ℨiii. decoque ex aq. fontan. ℥xii ad ℥vi colaturæ adde Tinctur. aromatic.
Syr. zinzib. aa ℥i. m. capt. cochl. duo larga secunda quaque hora ad quartam vicem nisi prius nausea supervenerit.

March 9th. He took four doses of the mixture without being in the least sick, and made, during the night upwards of two quarts of natural coloured water.

10th. Took the remainder of the mixture yesterday afternoon and evening, and was sick for a short time, but made nearly the same quantity of water as before, the swellings are considerably diminished, his appetite increased, but he is still costive.

R. Argent, viv. balsam peruv. aa ℨss tere ad extinctionem merc. et adde gum. ammon. ℈iii aloes socotorin. ℨss rad. scil. recent. ℈ss syr. simpl. q. s. f. mass. in pil. xxxii divid. cap. iii. bis in die.

14th. Continues to make water freely. The swellings of his legs have gradually decreased; soreness and tension of the abdomen considerably less.

Omittant. pil. cap. mistur. c. decoct. Digitalis. &c. 3tia quaque hora ad 3tiam vicem.

15th. Made a pint and a half of water last night, without being in the least sick, and is in every respect considerably better. Repet. Pillul. ut antea.

21st. Makes water as usual when in health, and the swellings are entirely gone.

R. Infus. amar. ℥v. tinctur. Rhei spirit. ℨii. spirit vitriol. dulc. ℨii. syr. zinzib. ℨvi. m. cap. cochl. iii. larg. ter in die.

He soon gained sufficient strength to enable him to go a journey, and returned home in much better health than he had been from the time he was affected with the paralytic stroke, and excepting some return of his asthmatic complaint in the winter, hath continued so ever since.

CASE II.

R—— Howgate, a man much addicted to intemperance, particularly in the use of spirituous liquors, Æt. 60, was admitted into the Hospital near Birmingham, May 17, 1783. He complained of difficulty of breathing, attended with cough, particularly troublesome on lying down; drowsiness and frequent dozing, from which he was roused by startings, accompanied with great anxiety and oppression about the breast; œdematous swellings of the legs; constant desire to make water, which he passed with difficulty, and only by drops; pulse weak and irregular; body rather costive; face much emaciated; no appetite for food.—Cap. pil. scil. iii. ter in die.

May 20th. The pills have had no effect.—Cap. mistur. c. Decoct. Digital. &c. cochl. ii. larg. 3tia quaque hora, ad 3tiam vicem.

May 21st. Made near two quarts of water in the night, without being in the least sick. He continued the use of the mixture three times in the day till the 30th, and made about three pints of water daily, by which means the swellings were entirely taken away; and his other complaints so much relieved, that on the 6th of June he was dismissed free from complaint, except a slight cough. But returning to his old course of life, he hath had frequent attacks of his disorder, which have been always removed by using the Digitalis.

Extract of a letter from Mr. Lyon, Surgeon, at Tamworth.

—Mr. Moggs was about 54 years of age, his disease a dropsy of the abdomen, attended with anasarcous swellings of the limbs, &c. brought on by excessive drinking. I believe the first symptoms of the disease appeared the beginning of November, 1776; the medicines he took before you saw him, were squills in different forms, sal diureticus and calomel, but without any good effect; he begun the Digitalis on the 10th of July 1777; a few doses of it caused a giddiness in the head, and almost deprived him of sight, with very great nausea, but very little vomiting, after which a considerable flow of urine ensued, and in a very short time, a very little water remained either in the cavity of the abdomen, or the membrana adiposa, but he remained excessive weak, with a fluttering pulse at the rate of 150 or frequently 160 in a minute; he kept pretty free from water for upwards of twelve months; it then collected, and neither the Digitalis nor any other medicine would carry it off. I tapped him the 2d of August 1779 in the usual place, and took some gallons of water from him, but he very soon filled again, and as he had a very large rupture, a considerable quantity of the water lodged in the scrotum, and could not be got away by tapping in the usual place. I therefore (on the 28th of the same month) made an incision into the lower part of the scrotum, and drained off all the water that way, but he was so very much reduced, that he died the 8th or 9th of September following, which was about two years and two months after he first begun the Digitalis.

I have had several dropsical patients relieved, and some perfectly recovered by the Digitalis, since you attended Mr. Moggs, but as I did not take any notes or make any memorandums of them, cannot give you any of them.

Communications from Dr. Stokes, Physician, in Stourbridge.

Dear Sir,

I accept with pleasure your invitation to communicate what I know respecting the properties of Digitalis; and if an account of what others had discovered before you, with a detail of my own experience, shall be allowed the merit of at least a well meant acknowledgment, for the early communication you were so kind to make me, of the valuable properties you had found in it; I shall consider my time as well employed. A knowledge of what has been already done is the best ground work of future experiment; on which account I have been the more full on this subject, in hopes that given with the cautions which you mean to lay down in the cure of dropsies, it may prove alike useful in that of other diseases, one of which stands foremost among the opprobria of medicine.

CASE I.

Mrs. M——. Orthopnea, pain, and excessive oppression at the bottom of the sternum. Pulse irregular, with frequent intermissions. Appetite very much impaired. Legs anasarcous.

Empl. vesicator. pectori dolent.
Infus. Digital. e ʒiii. ad. aq. &c. ʒviii. cochl. j. o. h. donec nausea excitetur vel diuresis satis copiosa proveniat.

I ordered it of the above strength, and to be repeated often, on account of the great emergency of the case, but the nausea excited by the first dose prevented its being given at such short intervals. A 3d dose I found had been given, which was followed by vomitings. All her complaints gradually abated, but in about a fortnight recurred, notwithstanding the use of infus. amar. &c.

Dec. 2. Infus. Digit. e. ʒiss ad aq. &c. ʒviii. cochl. ii. horis &c. u. a.

Complaints gradually abated, swellings of the legs nearly gone down.

About a month afterwards you was desired to visit this patient.

On the examination of the body I noticed, among others, the following appearances.

About ¾ oz. of bloody water flowed out, on elevating the upper half of the scull, and a small quantity also was found at the base.

Brain. Blood-vessels turgid with blood, and many of those of considerable size distended with air.

A very slight watery effusion between the Pia Mater and Tunica arachnoidea. About ¼ oz. of watery fluid in the lateral ventricles.

Thorax. In the left cavity about 4 oz. of bloody serum; in the right but little. Lungs, the hinder parts loaded with blood. Adhesions of each lobe to the pleura. Pericardium containing but a very small quantity of fluid. Heart containing no coagula of blood. Valves of the Aorta of a cartilaginous texture, as if beginning to ossify.

Abdominal Viscera natural, and a profusion of Fat under the integuments of the abdomen and thorax, in the former to the thickness of an inch and upwards, and in very considerable quantity on the mesentery, omentum, kidneys, &c.

Obs. The intermitting pulse should seem to have been owing to effusions of water in some of the cavities of the breast, as it disappeared on the removal of the waters.

CASE II.

Mrs. C—— of K——, Æt. 80. Orthopnœa, with sense of oppression about the prœcordia. Unable to lie down in bed for some nights past. Anasarca of the lower extremities. Urine very scanty. Complaints of six weeks standing. Had taken sal. diuret. c. ol. junip.—Calom. c. jalap, et gambog.—Et ol. junip. c. ol. Terebinth. without effect.

Feb. 7. Infus. Digital. e. ʒiii. ad aq. &c. ʒviii. cochl. ii. 4tis horis. Ordered to drink largely of infus. baccar. junip. The third dose produced great nausea which continued ten hours, during which time the urine made was about a quart. The next day her apothecary directed her to begin again with it. The second dose produced vomiting. During the next twenty hours she made two quarts of water, about four times as much as she drank.

From this time she took no more of the infus. Digital. but continued the inf. bacc. junip. until about March 2d, when all the swellings were gone down, her respiration perfectly free, and she herself quite restored to her former state of health. On the 29th she had an attack of jaundice which was some time after removed; since which she has enjoyed a good state of health, excepting that for some little time past her ancles have been slightly œdematous, which will I trust soon yield to strengthening medicines.

CASE III.

Mrs. M—— G——, Æt. 64. Has had sore legs for these thirty-four years past. Orthopnœa. Sense of oppression at the prœcordia. Pulse intermitting. Legs anasarcous. Urine scanty, high-coloured.

Infus. Digital. c. ʒiss ad aq. bull. ʒviii. cochl. ii. 4tis horis.

Took six doses, when nausea was excited. Urine a quart during the course of the night. The flow of urine continued, and complaints relieved. Sal. Mart. c. extr. gent. and afterwards with the addition of extr. cort. for which last ingredient she had a predilection, confirmed the cure.

On the same day the next year I was called in to her for a similar train of symptoms, excepting that the pulse was but just perceptibly irregular.

Infus. Digital. u. a. præscript.

The directions on the phial not being attended to, two doses of it were given after a nausea had been excited, which, with occasional vomitings, became exceedingly oppressive. A saline draught, given in Dr. Hulme's method, a draught sal. c. c. gr. xii. c. conf. card. gr. x. produced no immediate effect, but the nausea gradually abating, inf. bacc. junip. was ordered; but this appeared to augment it, and a great propensity to sleep coming on, I directed sal. c. c. conf. card, aa gr. viii. 4tis horis, which removed the unpleasant symptoms and myrrh. c. sal. mart. completed the cure. During the use of the above medicines, the urine was augmented, and the pulmonary complaints removed, even before the nausea left her; and the sores of her legs which were much inflamed before she began with the infus. Digital. in a day's time assumed a much healthier appearance, and on her other complaints going off, they shewed a greater tendency to heal than she had ever observed in them for twenty years before. This instance is a very pleasing confirmation of the experience of Hulse and Dr. Baylies, and of the advantage to be derived from a medicine, which, while it helps to heal the ulcers, removes that from the constitution which often renders the healing of them improper.

In one case in which I ordered it, the infusion, instead of digesting three hours as I had directed, was suffered to stand upon the leaves all night. The consequence was that the first dose produced considerable nausea.

The two following cases, with which I have been favoured by a physician very justly eminent, convince me of the necessity there is that every one who discovers a new medicine, or new virtues in an old one, should, in announcing such discoveries, publish to the world the exact manner in which he exhibits such medicines, with all the precautions necessary to obtain the promised success.

In these (says my correspondent) "the infusion was given in small doses, repeated every hour or two, till a nausea was raised, when it was omitted for a day or perhaps two, and then repeated in the same manner.

"An Ascites emptied by it, but filled again very speedily, though its use was never discontinued, and who afterwards found no salutary effects from it. Ended fatally.

"In an Anasarca it sometimes increased the quantity of urine, and abated the swelling, but which as often returned in as great a degree as before, though the medicine was still given, and always increased in quantity so as to excite nausea. Ended fatally.

"I have tried it in many other cases, but found very little difference in the success attending it."

May we not be allowed to conjecture that the inefficacy of its continued use is owing to its narcotic property gradually diminishing the irritability of the muscular fibres of the absorbents, or possibly of the whole vascular system, and thus adding to that weakened action which seems to be the cause of the generality of dropsies, which leads us to caution the medical experimenter against trying it, at least against its continued use, even in small doses, in other diseases of diminished energy, as continued fever, palsy, &c.

I remain with the greatest truth,
Your obliged and affectionate friend,
JONATHAN STOKES.

Stourbridge,
May 17, 1785.

The three following Hospital Cases, which Dr. Stokes had an opportunity of observing, are related as instances of bad practice, and tend to demonstrate how necessary it is when one physician adopts the medicine of another, that he should also at first rigidly adopt his method.

CASE I.

Esther K——, Æt. 33. General anasarca, ascites, and dyspnœa, of seven months duration.

Decoct. c Digit. ℥iv. c. aq. ℔i. coquend. ad ℔ss. cap. ℥i. 2dis. horis. 1st Day. 4th dose made her sick. 2d Day. The first dose she took to-day produced vomiting.

3d Day. Minuatur dosis ad ℥ss. This stayed upon her stomach, but produced an almost constant sickness. Stools more frequent, water scarce sensibly increased; and her swellings not at all reduced.

4th Day. Cap. Calomel. gambog. scill. &c.

Obs. Sufficient time was not allowed to observe its effects, neither was the patient enjoined the free use of diluents. The disease terminated fatally.

CASE II.

William T——, Æt. 42. Ascites, with cough and dyspnœa. Abdomen very much distended. The rest of his body highly emaciated. Urine thick, high coloured, and in very small quantity.

Decoct. Digit. (u. in Esther K——,) 4tis horis.

1st Day of taking it. The 4th dose produced sickness.

2d. Vomiting after the second dose.

10th. Urine increased to ℔vi.

11th. Flow of urine continues. Abdomen quite flaccid.

12th. Abdomen not diminished.

15th: A smart purging came on, and the flow of urine diminished.

23d. Belly much bound. Took a cathart. powder, which was followed by a diminution of the abdomen.

29th. To take a cathart. powder every 4th morning, continuing the decoct. Digit.

32d. Urine exceedingly scanty.

35th. Vin. scill. ʒss. o. m. &c. This produced diuretic effects.

44th. Tapped. Terminated fatally.

Obs. Here the medicine was continued till it ceased to produce diuretic effects; and these effects were not aided by any strengthening remedies.

CASE III.

George R——, Æt. 52. Ascites, general anasarca, and dyspnœa. His legs so greatly distended that it was with great difficulty he could draw the one after the other.

Infus. Digital. ʒiiiss. ad. aq. ℔ss. cap. ʒi. altern. horis donec nauseam excitaverit. Rep. 3tiis diebus. tempore intermedio cap. sol. guaic. ʒi. ter in die ex inf. sinap.

1st Day of taking it. Became sickish towards night.

2d Day. Made a great quantity of water during the night, and spat up a great deal of watery phlegm. The first dose he took in the morning has produced a sickness which has continued all day, but he has never vomited.

3d. Day. The change in his appearance so great as to make it difficult to conceive him to be the same person. Instead of a large corpulent man, he appeared tall, thin, and rather aged. Breathes freely, and can walk up and down stairs without inconvenience.

4th Day. Decoct. bacc. junip. and cyder for common drink.

6th Day. A second course of his medicine produced a flow of urine almost as plentiful as the former, though he drank little or nothing at the time. In a day or two after he walked to some distance.

12th Day. Pot. purgans illico.

14th Day. Pot. purg. c. jalap. ʒss. 4tis diebus.
Infus. Dig. 3tiis diebus.

17th Day. R. Gamb. gr. iii. calom. gr. ii. camph. gr. i. syr. simpl. fiat pil. o. n. sum.
Infus. Digit. 3tiis diebus.

21st Day. Made an out-patient. The super-abundant flow of urine continued for the first three days after his last course; but since, the flow of saliva has been nearly equal to that of urine.

The smalls of his legs not quite reduced, and are fuller at night. He has shrunk round the middle from four feet two inches to three feet six inches; and in the calves of his legs, from seventeen inches to thirteen and a half.

Obs. The waters were here very successfully evacuated, but as you remarked to me, on communicating the case to you at the time, tonic medicines should have been given, to second the ground that had been gained, instead of weakening the patient by drastic purgatives.

A CASE from Mr. Shaw, Surgeon, at Stourbridge.—Communicated by Doctor Stokes.

Matth. D——, Æt. 71. Tall and thin. Disease a general anasarca, with great difficulty of breathing. The lac ammoniac. somewhat relieved his breath; but the swellings increased, and his urine was not augmented. I considered it as a lost case, but having seen the good effects of the Digitalis, as ordered by Dr. Stokes in the case of Mrs. G——, I gave him one spoonful of an infusion of ʒii to half a pint, twice a day. His breath became much easier, his urine increased considerably, and the swellings gradually disappeared; since which his health has been pretty good, except that about three weeks ago, he had a slight dyspnœa, with pain in his stomach, which were soon removed by a repetition of the same medicine.

Mr. Shaw likewise informs me, that he has removed pains in the stomach and bowels, by giving a spoonful of the infusion, ʒiss. to ʒviii. morning and night.

A Letter from Mr. Vaux, Surgeon, in Birmingham.

Dear Sir,

I send you the two following cases, wherein the Digitalis had very powerful and sensible effects, in the cure of the different patients.

CASE I.

Mrs. O—— of L—— street, in this town, aged 28, naturally of a thin, spare habit, and her family inclinable to phthisis, sent for me on the 11th of June, 1779, at which time she complained of great pain in her side, a constant cough, expectorated much, which sunk in water; had colliquative sweats and frequent purging stools; the lower extremities and belly full of water, and from the great difficulty she had in breathing, I concluded there was water in the chest also. The quantity of water made at a time for three weeks before I saw her, never amounted to more than a tea-cup full, frequently not so much. Finding her in so alarming a situation, I gave it as my opinion she could receive no benefit from medicine, and requested her not to take any; but she being very desirous of my ordering her something, I complied, and sent her a box of gum pills with squills, and a mixture with salt of tartar: these medicines she took until the sixteenth, without any good effects: the water in her legs now began to exsude through the skin, and a small blister on one of her legs broke. Believing she could not exist much longer, unless an evacuation of the water could be procured; after fully informing her of her situation, and the uncertainty of her surviving the use of the medicine, I ventured to propose her taking the Digitalis, which she chearfully agreed to. I accordingly sent her a pint mixture, made as under, of the fresh leaves of the Digitalis. Three drams infused in one pint of boiling water, when cold strained off, without pressing the leaves, and two ounces of the strong juniper water added to it: of this mixture she was ordered four table spoonfuls every third hour, till it either made her sick, purged her, or had a sensible effect on the kidneys. This mixture was sent on the seventeenth, and she began taking it at noon on the eighteenth. At one o'clock the following morning I was called up, and informed she was dying. I immediately attended her, and was agreeably surprised to find their fright arose from her having fainted, in consequence of the sudden loss of twelve quarts of water she had made in about two hours. I immediately applied a roller round her belly, and, as soon as they could be made, 2 others, which were carried from the toes quite up the thighs. The relief afforded by these was immediate; but the medicine now began to affect her stomach so much, that she kept nothing on it many minutes together. I ordered her to drink freely of beef tea, which she did, but kept it on her stomach but a very short time. A neutral draught in a state of effervescence was taken to no good purpose: She therefore continued the beef tea, and took no other medicine for five days, when her sickness went off: her cough abated, but the pain in her side still continuing, I applied a blister which had the desired effect: her urine after the first day flowed naturally. Her cure was compleated by the gum pills with steel and the bitter infusion. It must be observed she never had any collection of water afterwards.

It affords me great pleasure to inform you that she is now living, and has since had four children; all of whom, I think I may justly say, are indebted to the Digitalis for their existence.

There appears in this case a striking proof of the utility of emetics in some kinds of consumptions, as it appears to me the dropsy was brought on by the cough, &c. and I believe these were cured by the continual vomitings, occasioned by the medicine.

CASE II.

Mr. H——, a publican, aged about 48 years, sent for me in March, 1778. He complained of a cough, shortness of breathing, which prevented him from laying down in bed; his belly, thighs and legs very much distended with water; the quantity of urine made at a time seldom exceeded a spoonful. I requested him to get some of the Digitalis, and as they had no proper weights in the house, I told them to put as much of the fresh leaves as would weigh down a guinea, into half a pint of boiling water; to let it stand till cold, then to pour off the clear liquor, and add a glass of gin to it, and to take three table spoonfuls every third hour, until it had some sensible effect upon him.

Before he had taken all the infusion, the quantity of urine made increased, (he therefore left off taking it), and it continued to do so until all the water was evacuated. His breathing became much better, his cough abated, though it never quite left him; he being for some time before asthmatic. By taking some tonic pills he continued quite well until the next spring, when he had a return of his complaint, which was carried off by the same means. Two years after, he had a third attack, and this also gave way to the medicine. Last year he died of a pleurisy.

I am, &c.
JER. VAUX

Moor-Street, 8th May,
1785.

P. S. You must well recollect the case of Mrs. F——.—It was "a general dropsy—every time she took the medicine its effects were similar, viz. The discharge of urine came on gradually at first, increased afterwards, and the whole of the water both in the belly, legs, &c. was perfectly evacuated. Although the effects were only temporary, they were exceedingly agreeable to the patient, making her time much more comfortable."—(See Case XLIII.)

A Letter from Mr. Wainwright, Surgeon, in Dudley.

Dear Sir,

It gives me great pleasure to find you intend to publish your observations on the Digitalis purpurea.

Several years are now elapsed since you communicated to me the high opinion you entertained of the diuretic qualities of this noble plant. To ensure success, due attention was recommended to its preparation, its dose, and its effects upon the system.

I always gave the infusion of the dried leaves; the dose the same as in the prescriptions returned. If the medicine operated on the stomach or bowels, it was thought prudent to forbear. When the kidneys began to perform their proper functions, and the urine to be discharged, a continuance of its farther use was unnecessary.

These remarks you made in the case of the first patient for whom you prescribed the Digitalis in our neighbourhood, and I have found them all necessary at this present period. From the decided good effects that followed from its use, in those cases where the most powerful remedies had failed, I was soon convinced it was a most valuable addition to the materia medica.

The want of a certain diuretic, has long been one of the desiderata of medicine. The Digitalis is undoubtedly at the head of that class, and will seldom, if properly administered, disappoint the expectation. I can speak with the more confidence, having, in an extensive practice, been a happy witness to its good qualities.

For several years, I have given the infusion in a variety of cases, where there was a deficiency in the secretion of the urine, with the greatest success. In recent obstructions, I do not recollect many failures. In anasarcous diseases, and in the anasarca, when combined with the ascites; in swellings of the limbs, and in diseases of the chest, when there was the greatest reason to believe an accumulation of serum, the most beneficial consequences have followed from its use.

Had I been earlier acquainted with your intention to publish an account of the Digitalis, I could have transmitted some cases, which might have served to corroborate these assertions: but I am convinced the Digitalis needs not my assistance to procure a favorable reception. Its own merit will ensure success, more than a hundred recited cases.

I could wish those gentlemen who intend to make use of this plant, to collect it in a hot dry day, when the petals fall, and the seed-vessels begin to swell.

The leaves kept to the second year are weaker, and their diuretic qualities much diminished. It will therefore be necessary to gather the plant fresh every season.

These cautions are unnecessary to the accurate botanist, who well knows, that a plant in the spring, though more succulent and full of juices, is destitute of those qualities which may be expected when that plant has attained its full vigour, and the seed-vessels begin to be manifest. But for want of attention to these particulars, its virtues may be thought exaggerated, or doubtful, if beneficial consequences do not always flow from its use. There are diseases it cannot cure; and in several of those patients in this town, who first took the Digitalis by your orders, there was the most positive proof of the viscera being unsound. In these desperate cases it often procured a plentiful flow of urine, and palliated a disease which medicine could not remove.

At a remote distance, physicians are seldom applied to for advice in trifling disorders. Many remedies have been tried without relief, and the disease is generally obstinate or confirmed.—It would not be fair to try the merits of the Digitalis in this scale. It might often fail of promoting the end desired. I flatter myself the reputation of this plant will be equal to its merit, and that it will meet with a candid reception.

As there is no pleasure equal to relieving the miseries and distresses of our fellow-creatures, I hope you will long enjoy that peculiar felicity.

Permit me to return my thankful acknowledgments, for your free communication of a medicine, by which means, through the blessing of providence, I have been enabled to restore health and happiness to many miserable objects.

I am, &c.
Yours,
J. WAINWRIGHT.

Dudley, April 26th, 1785.

CASE of Mr. Ward, Surgeon, in Birmingham.—Related by himself.

In September, 1782, I was seized with a difficulty of breathing, and oppression in my chest, in consequence of taking cold from being called out in the night. My tongue was foul; my urine small in quantity; my breath laborious and distressing on the slightest exercise. I tried the medicines most generally recommended, such as emetics, blisters, lac ammoniacum, oxymel of squills, &c. but finding little or no relief, I consulted Dr. Withering, who advised me to try the following prescription.

R. Fol. Digital. purp. siccat. ʒiss.
Aq. bullientis ℥iv.
Aq. cinn. sp. ℥ss. digere per horas quatuor, et colaturæ capiat cochlear. i. nocte maneque.

He also desired me to take fifty drops of tincture of cantharides three or four times a day.

After taking eight ounces of the infusion, and about twelve drams of the drops, I was perfectly cured, and have had no return since. The medicine did not occasion sickness or vertigo, nor had they any other sensible effect than in changing the appearance, and increasing the quantity of the urine, and rendering the tongue clean. After the last dose or two indeed, I had a little nausea, which was immediately removed by a small glass of brandy.

Birmingham, 1st July, 1785.

Communications from Mr. Yonge, Surgeon, in Shiffnall, Shropshire.

Dear Sir,

I have great satisfaction in complying with your just claim, by transcribing outlines of the subsequent cases, for insertion in your long requested tract on the Digitalis purpurea. The two first of these you will easily recollect, the cures having been conducted immediately under your own management, and the whole may add to that weight of evidence which long experience enables you to adduce of the efficacy of that valuable medicine. I have recited the only instances of its failure which occur to me, but many other, though successful cases, wherein its utility might seem dubious, and also the accounts received from people whose accuracy might be suspected, I shall not for obvious reasons trouble you with.

I am, dear Sir,
Your obliged friend,
WILLIAM YONGE.

Shiffnall,
May 1, 1785.

CASE I.

A Gentleman aged 49, on the night of the 21st of August, 1784, awaked with a sense of suffocation, which obliged him to rise up suddenly in bed. I found him complaining of difficult respiration, particularly on lying down; the countenance pale, and the pulse smaller and quicker than usual. Some brandy and water having been given, the symptoms gradually abated, so that he slept in a half recumbent posture. The following day he expressed a sense of anxiety and weight in the chest, attended by quicker breathing upon motion of the body. That evening an emetic of ipecacoanha was given, and afterwards a draught, with vitriolic æther and confect. card. aa ʒi to be repeated as the symptoms should require it. He continued to be affected with slighter returns of the dyspnœa at irregular intervals, until September 15th, when upon a more severe attack, the emetic was repeated. He now recollected some slight pain in his arms which had affected him previous to this last seizure, and was disposed to consider his complaint as rheumatic. Pills with gum ammoniac. gum guaiac. and antimonial powder were directed, with infus. amar. simpl. twice a day. The bowels were regulated by aperient pills of pulv. jalap. aloes and sal. tartar. and ʒiss balsam peruv. was given occasionally to alleviate the paroxysms of dyspnœa.

From this period until the beginning of November, little amendment or variation happened, except that respiration became more permanently difficult, and particularly oppressed upon motion, nor was it relieved by the expectoration of a mucous discharge, which now increased considerably. Squills, musk, ol. succini, æther, with other medicines of the same kind, were now used, but without success. The effects of opium and venæfection were tried. The appetite diminished, and his sleep became short and disturbed. He sometimes slept lying upon his back, but generally upon his left side. The urine which had hitherto been of good colour, and sufficient quantity, now became diminished, and lateritious; and the ancles œdematous.

On the 15th of November a blister was laid over the sternum, and ʒiss of oxymel scillitic. was given every eight hours.

On the 18th, a more copious discharge of urine took place; the swelling of the feet soon disappeared, and the respiration became gradually relieved.

On the 30th ʒi tinct. cantharidum twice a day in pyrmont water, with pills of ammoniac, sal tartar. et extract. gentian. were substituted, but

On the 7th of December, from some symptoms of relapse, the oxymel was used as before, and continued to be taken until the 27th, in doses as large as could be dispensed with on account of the great nausea which attended its exhibition: The urine was made in the quantity of four or five pints each day, during the whole time; the quantity then drank being seldom more than three pints. But now the sickness being exceedingly depressing, the strength failing, and the diuretic effects beginning to cease, the following prescription was directed.

R. Fol. Digitalis purpur. pulv. Ɪss. Spec. Aromatic. Ɪi. sp. lav. c. f. pilul. no. x. capiat i. nocte maneque, et alternis diebus sensim augeatur dosin.

In three days the effect of this medicine became visible, and when the dose of the Digitalis had been increased to six grains per day, the flow of urine generally amounted to seven pints every twenty-four hours. Not the least sickness, nor any other disagreeable symptom supervened, though he persevered in this plan until the end of January at which time the dyspnœa was removed, and he has continued gradually to regain his flesh, strength, and appetite, without any relapse.

CASE II.

About the middle of the year 1784 a lady aged 48, returned from London, to her native air in Shropshire, under symptoms of complicated disease. It was your opinion that the plethoric state, consequent to that period, when menstruation first begins to cease, had under various appearances, laid the foundation of that deplorable state which now presented itself. The skin was universally of a pale, leaden colour; her person much emaciated, and her strength so reduced, as to disable her from walking without support. The appetite fluctuating, the digestion impaired so much, that solids passed the intestines with little appearance of solution: She had generally eight or ten alvine evacuations every day, and without this number, febrile symptoms, attended with severe vertiginous affection, and vomiting regularly ensued. The stools were of a pale ash colour. The urine generally pale, and at first in due quantity. The region of the stomach had a tense feel, without soreness: the feet and ancles œdematous, her sleep was uncertain: the pulse varying between 94 and 100, and feeble, except upon the approach of the menstrual periods, which were now only marked by its increased strength, and exacerbation of other febrile symptoms. Emetics, saline medicines, and gentle aperients were necessary to alleviate these. Six grains of ipecac, operated with sufficient power, and half a grain of calomel would have purged with great violence.

From the time of her arrival till the middle of August, mercury had been continued in various forms, and in doses such as the irritable state of her stomach and bowels would admit of. Spirit. nitri dulc.; sal. tartar, squill, and cantharides were alternately employed as diuretics, but without success, to retard the progress of an universal anasarca which was then advanced to such degree and accompanied by so great debility, and other dreadful concomitants, as to threaten a speedy and fatal catastrophe.

On the 16th of August you first saw her, and directed thus.

R. Mercur. cinerei gr. ii.
Fol. Digital, purpur. pulv. ℈i. f. mass. in pill. no. xvi. dividend.—sumat unam hora meridiana, iterumque hora quinta pomeridiana quotidie.

Capiat lixivii saponac. gutt. L. in haust. juscul. sine sale parati omni nocte.

On the 20th the flow of urine began to increase, and she continued the medicine in the same dose until the 20th of September, discharging from six to eight pints of water each day for the first week, and which quantity gradually diminished as she became empty. During this period she complained not of any sickness, except from the lixivium, which was after the first dose reduced to 20 drops; and her appetite and strength increased daily, though it was evident that no bile had yet flowed into the bowels, nor was the digestion at all improved. The anasarcous appearances being then removed, the Digitalis was omitted, and pills, composed of mercur. cinereus, aloes, and sal tartari directed twice a day, with ʒi. of vin. chalybeat. in infus. amar. simpl.

Her amendment in other respects proceeded slowly, but regularly, from that time until the 9th of October; when the state of plethora again recurring, with its usual attendant symptoms, ʒiv. of blood were taken from the arm; and this was upon the same occasion, repeated in the following month, with manifest good consequences; though in both instances the colour of the blood, as flowing from the vein could hardly be called red, and the coagulum was as weak in its cohesion as possible. The state of the stomach and bowels was by this time greatly improved, in common with other parts of the system; but no intromission of bile had yet happened: the hardness about the hypogastric region, though less, continued in a considerable degree, and you ordered pills of mercury rubbed down, and rust of iron, to be taken twice a day, with a decoction of dandelion and sal sodæ.

A cataplasm of linseed was applied every night over the stomach and right side; and, with little deviation from this plan, she continued to the end of the year, improving in her general health, but the hepatic affection yet remaining. It was then determined to try the effects of electricity, and gentle shocks were passed through the body daily, and as nearly as could be through the liver, in various directions.

On the fifth day there was reason to think that some gall had been secreted and poured out, and this became every day more evident; but it flowed only in small quantity, and irregularly into the bowels, as appeared from the fæces being partially tinged by it.

In February the lady left this neighbourhood, and though convalescent, yet so nearly well as to promise us the satisfaction of seeing her perfectly restored.

June 29. The bile is now secreted in pretty good quantity, her appetite is perfectly good, her strength equal to almost any degree of exercise, and her health in general better than it has been for some years.

CASE III.

Mr. W——, aged—. In June, 1782, was affected with slight difficulty in respiration, upon taking exercise or lying down in bed. These symptoms increased gradually until the end of July, when he complained of sense of weight and uneasiness about the prœcordia; loss of appetite; and costiveness. The urine was small in quantity, and high coloured; his pulse feeble, and intermitting; he breathed with difficulty when in bed, and slept little. After the exhibition of an emetic, and an opening medicine of rhubarb, sena, and sal tartari, he was directed to take half a dram of squill pill, pharm. Edinburg. night and morning, with ℨss sal. sodæ in ℥iss. infus. amar. simpl. twice a day; and these medicines were continued during ten days, without any sensible effect. A blister was then applied to the sternum, and six grains of calomel given in the evening. The symptoms were now increased very considerably, in every particular; and the following infusion was substituted for the former medicines.

R. Fol. Digital. purpur. ℨiii.
Cort. limon. ℨii. infund.
Aq. bullient. ℔i. per hor. 2 et cola. sumat cochl. i. primo mane et repet. omni hora.

Sometime in the night considerable nausea occurred, and the following day he began to make water in great quantity, which he continued to do for three or four days. The pulse in a few hours became regular, slower, and stronger, and, in the course of a week, all the symptoms entirely vanished, and an electuary of cort. peruvian, sal martis, and spec. aromatic. confirmed his cure.

In February, 1784, this gentleman had a relapse of his disease, from which he again soon recovered by the same means, and is now perfectly well.

CASE IV.

G—— A——, a husbandman, aged 57. Was in the year 1782 affected with a slight, but constant pain in his breast, with difficult respiration. His countenance was yellow; the abdomen swelled, and hard; his urine high coloured, and in small quantity; appetite and sleep little. Complained of frequent nausea, and of sudden profuse sweatings, which seemed for a short time to relieve the dyspnœa.

After the exhibition of an emetic, six grains of calomel were given, with a purge of jalap in the morning, and repeated in a few days, with some appearance of advantage. He was then directed to take some pills of squill, soap, and rhubarb, with a draught twice a day, consisting of infus. amar. simp. and sal tartari. The skin soon became clearer and the pain in his breast considerably diminished. But every other circumstance remaining the same, and a fluctuation in the belly being now more evident, the infusion of Digitalis as prescribed in case third, was given in the dose of one ounce twice a day.

On the 5th day the effects were apparent, and he continued his medicine for a fortnight without nausea, making four or five pints of water every night, but little in the day, and gradually losing the symptoms of his disease.

In 1784, this person had a relapse, and was again cured by similar treatment.

CASE V.

R—— H——, Aged 43. Towards the end of the year 1783, became affected with slight cough and expectoration of purulent matter. In December his skin became universally of a pale yellow colour. The abdomen was swelled and hard; his appetite little, and he complained of a violent and constant palpitation of the heart, which prevented him from sleeping. The urine pale, and in small quantity. The pulse exceedingly strong, and rebounding; beating 114 to 120 strokes every minute. He suffered violent pain of his head, and was very feeble and emaciated. After bleeding, and the use of gentle aperient medicines, he continued to take the infusion of Digitalis for some days, without any sensible effect. Other diuretics were tried to as little purpose. Repeated bleeding had no effect in diminishing the violent action of the heart. He died in January following, under complicated symptoms of phthisis and ascites.

CASE VI.

A man aged 57, who had lived freely in the summer of 1784, became affected with œdematous swelling of his legs, for which he was advised to drink Fox Glove Tea. He took a four ounce bason of the infusion made strong with the green leaves, every morning for four successive days.

On the 5th he was suddenly seized with faintness and cold sweatings. I found him with a pale countenance, complaining of weakness, and of pain, with a sense of great heat in his stomach and bowels. The swelling of the legs was entirely gone, he having evacuated urine in very large quantities for the two preceding days. He was affected with frequent diarrhœa. The pulse was very quick and small, and his extremities cold.

A small quantity of broth was directed to be given him every half hour, and blisters were applied to the ancles, by which his symptoms became gradually alleviated, and he recovered perfectly in the space of three weeks; except a relapse of the anasarca, for which the Digitalis was afterwards successfully employed, in small doses, without any disagreeable consequence.

CASE VII.

S—— D——, a middle aged single woman, was affected in the year eighty-one, with a painful rigidity and slight inflammation of the integuments on the left side, extending from the ear to the shoulder. In every other particular she was healthy. The use of warm fomentations, and opium, with two or three doses of mercurial physic, afforded her ease and the inflammation disappeared, but was succeeded by an œdematous swelling of the part, which very gradually extended along the arm, and downward to the breast, back, and belly. Friction, electricity and mercurial ointment were amongst the number of applications unsuccessfully employed to relieve her for the space of three months, during which time she continued in good general health.

In November she became ascitic, passing small quantities of urine, and soon afterwards a sudden dyspnœa gave occasion to suppose an effusion of water in the thorax. The Digitalis, squills, and cantharides were given in very considerable doses without effect. She died the latter end of December following.

CASE VIII.

W—— C——, a collier aged 58, was attacked in the spring of 1783 with a tertian ague, which he attributed to cold, by sleeping in a coal pit, and from which he recovered in a few days, except a swelling of the lower extremities, which had appeared about that time, and gradually increased for two or three months. The legs and thighs were greatly enlarged and œdematous. His belly was swelled, but no fluctuation perceptible. He made small quantities of high coloured water. The appetite bad, and pulse feeble. He had taken many medicines without relief, and was now so reduced in strength, as to sit up with difficulty. An infusion of the Digitalis was directed for him, in the proportion of one ounce of the fresh leaves to a pint of water, two ounces to be taken three times a day, until the stomach or bowels became affected. Upon the exhibition of the sixth dose, nausea supervened, and continued to oppress him at intervals for two or three days, during which he passed large quantities of pale urine. The swelling, assisted by moderate bandage rapidly diminished, and without any repetition of his medicine, at the expiration of sixteen days, he returned to his labour perfectly recovered.

FOOTNOTES:

R. Rad. scil. recent. sapon. castiliens. pulv. Rhei opt. aa. ϶i. ol. junip. gutt. xvi. syr. bals. q. s. f. mass. in pil. xxiv. divid.

Prepared in the same manner as in the former case.

See this account in the Introduction.

For reasons assigned at p. 100, I did not intend to introduce any case, occurring under my own inspection, in the course of the present year; but it may be satisfactory to continue the history of this disease, as Dr. Stokes's narrative would otherwise be incomplete.

1785.

CASE.

Jan. 5th. Mrs. M——, Æt. 48. Hydrothorax and anasarcous legs, of eight months duration. She had taken jallap, squill, salt of tartar, and various other medicines. I found her in a very reduced state, and therefore directed only a grain and half of the Pulv. Digital. to be given night and morning. This in a few days encreased the secretion of urine, removed her difficulty of breathing, and reduced the swelling of her legs, without any disturbance to her system.

Three months afterwards, a severe attack of gout in her legs and arms, removing to her head, she died.

Dr. Stokes had an opportunity of examining the dead body, and I had the satisfaction to learn from him, that there did not appear to have been any return of the dropsy.

In the three last recited cases, the medicine was directed in doses quite too strong, and repeated too frequently. If Esther K—— could have survived the extreme sickness, the diuretic effects would probably have taken place, and, from her time of life, I should have expected a recovery. Wm. T—— seems to have been a bad case, and I think would not have been cured under any management. G. R—— certainly possessed a good constitution, or he must have shared the fate of the other two.

OF THE PREPARATIONS and DOSES, OF THE FOXGLOVE

Every part of the plant has more or less of the same bitter taste, varying, however, as to strength, and changing with the age of the plant and the season of the year.

ROOT.—This varies greatly with the age of the plant. When the stem has shot up for flowering, which it does the second year of its growth, the root becomes dry, nearly tasteless, and inert.

Some practitioners, who have used the root, and been so happy as to cure their patients without exciting sickness, have been pleased to communicate the circumstance to me as an improvement in the use of the plant. I have no doubt of the truth of their remarks, and I thank them. But the case of Dr. Cawley puts this matter beyond dispute. The fact is, they have fortunately happened to use the root in its approach to its inert state, and consequently have not over dosed their patients. I could, if necessary, bring other proof to shew that the root is just as capable as the leaves, of exciting nausea.

STEM.—The stem has more taste than the root has, in the season the stem shoots out, and less taste than the leaves. I do not know that it has been particularly selected for use.

LEAVES.—These vary greatly in their efficacy at different seasons of the year, and, perhaps, at different stages of their growth; but I am not certain that this variation keeps pace with the greater or lesser intensity of their bitter taste.

Some who have been habituated to the use of the recent leaves, tell me, that they answer their purpose at every season of the year; and I believe them, notwithstanding I myself have found very great variations in this respect. The solution of this difficulty is obvious. They have used the leaves in such large proportion, that the doses have been sufficient, or more than sufficient, even in their most inefficacious state. The Leaf-stalks seem, in their sensible properties, to partake of an intermediate state between the leaves and the stem.

FLOWERS.—The petals, the chives, and the pointal have nearly the taste of the leaves, and it has been suggested to me, by a very sensible and judicious friend, that it might be well to fix on the flower for internal use. I see no objection to the proposition; but I have not tried it.

SEEDS.—These I believe are equally untried.

From this view of the different parts of the plant, it is sufficiently obvious why I still continue to prefer the leaves.

These should be gathered after the flowering stem has shot up, and about the time that the blossoms are coming forth.

The leaf-stalk and mid-rib of the leaves should be rejected, and the remaining part should be dried, either in the sun-shine, or on a tin pan or pewter dish before a fire.

If well dried, they readily rub down to a beautiful green powder, which weighs something less than one-fifth of the original weight of the leaves. Care must be taken that the leaves be not scorched in drying, and they should not be dried more than what is requisite to allow of their being readily reduced to powder.

I give to adults, from one to three grains of this powder twice a day. In the reduced state in which physicians generally find dropsical patients, four grains a day are sufficient. I sometimes give the powder alone; sometimes unite it with aromatics, and sometimes form it into pills with a sufficient quantity of soap or gum ammoniac.

If a liquid medicine be preferred, I order a dram of these dried leaves to be infused for four hours in half a pint of boiling water, adding to the strained liquor an ounce of any spirituous water. One ounce of this infusion given twice a day, is a medium dose for an adult patient. If the patient be stronger than usual, or the symptoms very urgent, this dose may be given once in eight hours; and on the contrary in many instances half an ounce at a time will be quite sufficient. About thirty grains of the powder or eight ounces of the infusion, may generally be taken before the nausea commences.

The ingenuity of man has ever been fond of exerting itself to vary the forms and combinations of medicines. Hence we have spirituous, vinous, and acetous tinctures; extracts hard and soft, syrups with sugar or honey, &c. but the more we multiply the forms of any medicine, the longer we shall be in ascertaining its real dose. I have no lasting objection however to any of these formulæ except the extract, which, from the nature of its preparation must ever be uncertain in its effects; and a medicine whose fullest dose in substance does not exceed three grains, cannot be supposed to stand in need of condensation.

It appears from several of the cases, that when the Digitalis is disposed to purge, opium may be joined with it advantageously; and when the bowels are too tardy, jalap may be given at the same time, without interfering with its diuretic effects; but I have not found benefit from any other adjunct.

From this view of the doses in which the Digitalis really ought to be exhibited, and from the evidence of many of the cases, in which it appears to have been given in quantities six, eight, ten or even twelve times more than necessary, we must admit as an inference either that this medicine is perfectly safe when given as I advise, or that the medicines in daily use are highly dangerous.

EFFECTS, RULES, and CAUTIONS

The Foxglove when given in very large and quickly-repeated doses, occasions sickness, vomiting, purging, giddiness, confused vision, objects appearing green or yellow; increased secretion of urine, with frequent motions to part with it, and sometimes inability to retain it; slow pulse, even as slow as 35 in a minute, cold sweats, convulsions, syncope, death.

When given in a less violent manner, it produces most of these effects in a lower degree; and it is curious to observe, that the sickness, with a certain dose of the medicine, does not take place for many hours after its exhibition has been discontinued; that the flow of urine will often precede, sometimes accompany, frequently follow the sickness at the distance of some days, and not unfrequently be checked by it. The sickness thus excited, is extremely different from that occasioned by any other medicine; it is peculiarly distressing to the patient; it ceases, it recurs again as violent as before; and thus it will continue to recur for three or four days, at distant and more distant intervals.

These sufferings of the patient are generally rewarded by a return of appetite, much greater than what existed before the taking of the medicine.

But these sufferings are not at all necessary; they are the effects of our inexperience, and would in similar circumstances, more or less attend the exhibition of almost every active and powerful medicine we use.

Perhaps the reader will better understand how it ought to be given, from the following detail of my own improvement, than from precepts peremptorily delivered, and their source veiled in obscurity.

At first I thought it necessary to bring on and continue the sickness, in order to ensure the diuretic effects.

I soon learnt that the nausea being once excited, it was unnecessary to repeat the medicine, as it was certain to recur frequently, at intervals more or less distant.

Therefore my patients were ordered to persist until the nausea came on, and then to stop. But it soon appeared that the diuretic effects would often take place first, and sometimes be checked when the sickness or a purging supervened.

The direction was therefore enlarged thus—Continue the medicine until the urine flows, or sickness or purging take place.

I found myself safe under this regulation for two or three years; but at length cases occurred in which the pulse would be retarded to an alarming degree, without any other preceding effect.

The directions therefore required an additional attention to the state of the pulse, and it was moreover of consequence not to repeat the doses too quickly, but to allow sufficient time for the effects of each to take place, as it was found very possible to pour in an injurious quantity of the medicine, before any of the signals for forbearance appeared.

Let the medicine therefore be given in the doses, and at the intervals mentioned above:—let it be continued until it either acts on the kidneys, the stomach, the pulse, or the bowels; let it be stopped upon the first appearance of any one of these effects, and I will maintain that the patient will not suffer from its exhibition, nor the practitioner be disappointed in any reasonable expectation.

If it purges, it seldom succeeds well.

The patients should be enjoined to drink very freely during its operation. I mean, they should drink whatever they prefer, and in as great quantity as their appetite for drink demands. This direction is the more necessary, as they are very generally prepossessed with an idea of drying up a dropsy, by abstinence from liquids, and fear to add to the disease, by indulging their inclination to drink.

In cases of ascites and anasarca; when the patients are weak, and the evacuation of the water rapid; the use of proper bandage is indispensably necessary to their safety.

If the water should not be wholly evacuated, it is best to allow an interval of several days before the medicine be repeated, that food and tonics maybe administered; but truth compels me to say, that the usual tonic medicines have in these cases very often deceived my expectations.

From some cases which have occurred in the course of the present year, I am disposed to believe that the Digitalis may be given in small doses, viz. two or three grains a day, so as gradually to remove a dropsy, without any other than mild diuretic effects, and without any interruption to its use until the cure be compleated.

If inadvertently the doses of the Foxglove should be prescribed too largely, exhibited too rapidly, or urged to too great a length; the knowledge of a remedy to counteract its effects would be a desirable thing. Such a remedy may perhaps in time be discovered. The usual cordials and volatiles are generally rejected from the stomach; aromatics and strong bitters are longer retained; brandy will sometimes remove the sickness when only slight; I have sometimes thought small doses of opium useful, but I am more confident of the advantage from blisters. Mr. Jones (Page 135) in one case, found mint tea to be retained longer than other things.

FOOTNOTES:

I am doubtful whether it does not sometimes excite a copious flow of saliva.—See cases at pages 115, 154, and 155.

CONSTITUTION of PATIENTS

Independent of the degree of disease, or of the strength or age of the patient, I have had occasion to remark, that there are certain constitutions favourable, and others unfavourable to the success of the Digitalis.

From large experience, and attentive observation, I am pretty well enabled to decide a priori upon this matter, and I wish to enable others to do the same: but I feel myself hardly equal to the undertaking. The following hints, however, aiding a degree of experience in others, may lead them to accomplish what I yet can describe but imperfectly.

It seldom succeeds in men of great natural strength, of tense fibre, of warm skin, of florid complexion, or in those with a tight and cordy pulse.

If the belly in ascites be tense, hard, and circumscribed, or the limbs in anasarca solid and resisting, we have but little to hope.

On the contrary, if the pulse be feeble or intermitting, the countenance pale, the lips livid, the skin cold, the swollen belly soft and fluctuating, or the anasarcous limbs readily pitting under the pressure of the finger, we may expect the diuretic effects to follow in a kindly manner.

In cases which foil every attempt at relief, I have been aiming, for some time past, to make such a change in the constitution of the patient, as might give a chance of success to the Digitalis.

By blood-letting, by neutral salts, by chrystals of tartar, squills, and occasional purging, I have succeeded, though imperfectly. Next to the use of the lancet, I think nothing lowers the tone of the system more effectually than the squill, and consequently it will always be proper, in such cases, to use the squill; for if that fail in its desired effect, it is one of the best preparatives to the adoption of the Digitalis.

A tendency to paralytic affections, or a stroke of the palsy having actually taken place, is no objection to the use of the Digitalis; neither does a stone existing in the bladder forbid its use. Theoretical ideas of sedative effects in the former, and apprehensions of its excitement of the urinary organs in the latter case, might operate so as to make us with-hold relief from the patient; but experience tells me, that such apprehensions are groundless.

INFERENCES.

To prevent any improper influence, which the above recitals of the efficacy of the medicine, aided by the novelty of the subject, may have upon the minds of the younger part of my readers, in raising their expectations to too high a pitch, I beg leave to deduce a few inferences, which I apprehend the facts will fairly support.

I. That the Digitalis will not universally act as a diuretic.

II. That it does do so more generally than any other medicine.

III. That it will often produce this effect after every other probable method has been fruitlessly tried.

IV. That if this fails, there is but little chance of any other medicine succeeding.

V. That in proper doses, and under the management now pointed out, it is mild in its operation, and gives less disturbance to the system, than squill, or almost any other active medicine.

VI. That when dropsy is attended by palsy, unsound viscera, great debility, or other complication of disease, neither the Digitalis, nor any other diuretic can do more than obtain a truce to the urgency of the symptoms; unless by gaining time, it may afford opportunity for other medicines to combat and subdue the original disease.

VII. That the Digitalis may be used with advantage in every species of dropsy, except the encysted.

VIII. That it may be made subservient to the cure of diseases, unconnected with dropsy.

IX. That it has a power over the motion of the heart, to a degree yet unobserved in any other medicine, and that this power may be converted to salutary ends.

PRACTICAL REMARKS ON DROPSY, AND SOME OTHER DISEASES

The following remarks consist partly of matter of fact, and partly of opinion. The former will be permanent; the latter must vary with the detection of error, or the improvement of knowledge. I hazard them with diffidence, and hope they will be examined with candour; not by a contrast with other opinions, but by an attentive comparison with the phœnomena of disease.

ANASARCA.

§ 1. The anasarca is generally curable when seated in the subcutaneous cellular membrane, or in the substance of the lungs.

§ 2. When the abdominal viscera in general are greatly enlarged, which they sometimes are, without effused fluid in the cavity of the abdomen; the disease is incurable. After death, the more solid viscera are found very large and pale. If the cavity contains water, that water may be removed by diuretics.

§ 3. In swollen legs and thighs, where the resistance to pressure is considerable, the tendency to transparency in the skin not obvious, and where the alteration of posture occasions but little alteration in the state of distension, the cure cannot be effected by diuretics.

Is this difficulty of cure occasioned by spissitude in the effused fluids, by want of proper communication from cell to cell, or is the disease rather caused by a morbid growth of the solids, than by an accumulation of fluid?

Is not this disease in the limbs similar to that of the viscera (§ 2)?

§ 4. Anasarcous swellings often take place in palsied limbs, in arms as well as legs; so that the swelling does not depend merely upon position.

§ 5. Is there not cause to suspect that many dropsies originate from paralytic affections of the lymphatic absorbents? And if so, is it not probable that the Digitalis, which is so effectual in removing dropsy, may also be used advantageously in some kinds of palsy?

ASCITES.

§ 6. If existing alone, (i. e.) without accompanying anasarca, is in children curable; in adults generally incurable by medicines. Tapping may be used here with better chance for success than in more complicated dropsies. Sometimes cured by vomiting.

ASCITES and ANASARCA.

§ 7. Incurable if dependant upon irremediably diseased viscera, or on a gouty constitution, so debilitated, that the gouty paroxysms no longer continue to be formed.

In every other situation the disease yields to diuretics and tonics.

ASCITES, ANASARCA, and HYDROTHORAX.

§ 8. Under this complication, though the symptoms admit of relief, the restoration of the constitution can hardly be hoped for.

ASTHMA.

§ 9. The true spasmodic asthma, a rare disease—is not relieved by Digitalis.

§ 10. In the greater part of what are called asthmatical cases, the real disease is anasarca of the lungs, and is generally to be cured by diuretics. (See § 1.) This is almost always combined with some swelling of the legs.

§ 11. There is another kind of asthma, in which change of posture does not much affect the patient. I believe it to be caused by an infarction of the lungs. It is incurable by diuretics; but it is often accompanied with a degree of anasarca, and so far it admits of relief.

Is not this disease similar to that in the limbs at (§ 3,) and also to that of the abdominal viscera at (§ 2.)?

ASTHMA and ANASARCA.

§ 12. If the asthma be of the kind mentioned at (§§ 9 and 11,) diuretics can only remove the accompanying anasarca. But if the affection of the breath depends also upon cellular effusion, as it mostly does, the patient may be taught to expect a recovery.

ASTHMA and ASCITES.

§ 13. A rare combination, but not incurable if the abdominal viscera are sound. The asthma is here most probably of the anasarcous kind (§ 10;) and this being seldom confined to the lungs only, the disease generally appears in the following form.

ASTHMA, ASCITES, and ANASARCA.

§ 14. The curability of this combination will depend upon the circumstances mentioned in the preceding section, taking also into the account the strength or weakness of the patient.

EPILEPSY.

§ 15. In epilepsy dependant upon effusion, the Digitalis will effect a cure; and in the cases alluded to, the dropsical symptoms were unequivocal. It has not had a sufficient trial in my hands, to determine what it can do in other kinds of epilepsy.

HYDATID DROPSY.

§ 16. This may be distinguished from common ascites, by the want of evident fluctuation. It is common to both sexes. It does not admit of a cure either by tapping or by medicine.

HYDROCEPHALUS.

§ 17. This disease, which has of late so much attracted the attention of the medical world, I believe, originates in inflammation; and that the water found in the ventricles of the brain after death, is the consequence, and not the cause of the illness.

It has seldom happened to me to be called upon in the earlier stages of this complaint, and the symptoms are at first so similar to those usually attendant upon dentition and worms, that it is very difficult to pronounce decidedly upon the real nature of the disease; and it is rather from the failure of the usual modes of relief, than from any other more decided observation, that we at length dare to give it a name.

At first, the febrile symptoms are sometimes so unsteady, that I have known them mistaken for the symptoms of an intermittent, and the cure attempted by the bark.

In the more advanced stages, the diagnostics obtrude themselves upon our notice, and put the situation of the patient beyond a doubt. But this does not always happen. The variations of the pulse, so accurately described by the late Dr. Whytt, do not always ensue. The dilatation of the pupils, the squinting, and the aversion to light, do not universally exist. The screaming upon raising the head from the pillow or the lap, and the flushing of the cheeks, I once considered as affording indubitable marks of the disease; but in a child which I sometime since attended with Dr. Ash, the pulse was uniformly about 85, (except during the first week, before we had the care of the patient.) The child never shewed any aversion to the light; never had dilated pupils, never squinted, never screamed when raised from the lap or taken out of the bed, nor did we observe any remarkable flushing of the cheeks; and the sleep was quiet, but sometimes moaning.

Frequent vomiting existed from the first, but ceased for several days towards the conclusion. One or two worms came away during the illness, and it was all along difficult to purge the child. Three days before death, the right side became slightly paralytic, and the pupil of that eye somewhat dilated.

After death, about two ounces and a half of water were found in the ventricles of the brain, and the vessels of the dura mater were turgid with blood.

If I am right as to the nature of hydrocephalus, that it is at first dependant upon inflammation, or congestion; and that the water in the ventricles is a consequence, and not a cause of the disease; the curative intentions ought to be extremely different in the first and the last stages.

It happens very rarely that I am called to patients at the beginning, but in two instances wherein I was called at first, the patients were cured by repeated topical bleedings, vomits, and purges.

Some years ago I mentioned these opinions, and the success of the practice resulting from them, to Dr. Quin, now physician at Dublin. That gentleman had lately taken his degree, and had chosen hydrocephalus for the subject of his thesis in the year 1779. In this very ingenious essay, which he gave me the same morning, I was much pleased to find that the author had not only held the same ideas relative to the nature of the disease, but had also confirmed them by dissections.

In the year 1781, another case in the first stage demanded my attention. The reader is referred back to Case LXIX for the particulars.

I have not yet been able to determine whether the Digitalis can or cannot be used with advantage in the second stage of the hydrocephalus. In Case XXXIII. the symptoms of death were at hand; in Case LXIX. the practice, though successful, was too complicated, and in Case CLI. the medicine was certainly stopped too soon.

When we consider what enormous quantities of mercury may be used in this complaint, without affecting the salivary glands, it seems probable that other parts may be equally insensible to the action of their peculiar stimuli, and therefore that the Digitalis ought to be given in much larger doses in this, than in other diseases.

HYDROTHORAX.

§ 18. Under this name I also include the dropsy of the pericardium.

The intermitting pulse, and pain in the arms, sufficiently distinguish this disease from asthma, and from anasarcous lungs.

It is very universally cured by the Digitalis.

§ 19. I lately met with two cases which had been considered and treated as angina pectoris. They both appeared to me to be cases of hydrothorax. One subject was a clergyman, whose strength had been so compleatly exhausted by the continuance of the disease, and the attempts to relieve it, that he did not survive many days. The other was a lady, whose time of life made me suspect effusion. I directed her to take small doses of the pulv. Digitalis, which in eight days removed all her complaints. This happened six months ago, and she remains perfectly well.

HYDROTHORAX and ANASARCA.

§ 20. This combination is very frequent, and, I believe, may always be cured by the Digitalis.

§ 21. Dropsies in the chest either with or without anasarcous limbs, are much more curable than those of the belly. Probably because the abdominal viscera are more frequently diseased in the latter than in the former cases.

INSANITY.

§ 22. I apprehend this disease to be more frequently connected with serous effusion than has been commonly imagined.

§ 23. Where appearances of anasarca point out the true cause of the complaint, as in cases XXIV. and XXXIV. the happiest effects may be expected from the Digitalis; and men of more experience than myself in cases of insanity, will probably employ it successfully in other less obvious circumstances.

NEPHRITIS CALCULOSA.

§ 24. We have had sufficient evidence of the efficacy of the Foxglove in removing the Dysuria and other symptoms of this disease; but probably it is not in these cases preferable to the tobacco.

OVARIUM DROPSY.

§ 25. This species of encysted dropsy is not without difficulty distinguishable from an ascites; and yet it is necessary to distinguish them, because the two diseases require different treatment and because the probality of a cure is much greater in one than in the other.

§ 26. The ovarium dropsy is generally slow in its progress; for a considerable time the patient though somewhat emaciated, does not lose the appearance of health, and the urine flows in the usual quantity. It is seldom that the practitioner is called in early enough to distinguish by the feel on which side the cyst originated, and the patients do not attend to that circumstance themselves. They generally menstruate regularly in the incipient state of the disease, and it is not until the pressure from the sac becomes very great, that the urinary secretion diminishes. In this species of dropsy, the patients, upon being questioned, acknowledge even from a pretty early date, pains in the upper and inner parts of the thighs, similar to those which women experience in a state of pregnancy. These pains are for a length of time greater in one thigh than in the other, and I believe it will be found that the disease originated on that side.

§ 27. The ovarium dropsy defies the power of medicine. It admits of relief, and sometimes of a cure, by tapping. I submit to the consideration of practitioners, how far we may hope to cure this disease by a seton or a caustic.—In the LXIst case the patient was too much reduced, and the disease too far advanced to allow of a cure by any method; but it teaches us that a caustic may be used with safety.

§ 28. When tapping becomes necessary, I always advise the adoption of the waistcoat bandage or belt, invented by the late very justly celebrated Dr. Monro, and described in the first volume of the Medical Essays. I also enjoin my patients to wear this bandage afterwards, from a persuasion that it retards the return of the disease. The proper use of bandage, when the disorder first discovers itself, certainly contributes much to prevent its increase.

OVARIUM DROPSY with ANASARCA.

§ 29. The anasarca does not appear until the encysted dropsy is very far advanced. It is then probably caused by weakness and pressure. The Digitalis removes it for a time.

PHTHISIS PULMONALIS.

§ 30. This is a very increasing malady in the present day. It is no longer limited to the middle part of life: children at five years of age die of it, and old people at sixty or seventy. It is not confined to the flat-chested, the fair-skinned, the blue eyed, the light-haired, or the scrophulous: it often attacks people with full chests, brown skins, dark hair and eyes, and those in whose family no scrophulous taint can be traced. It is certainly infectious. The very strict laws still existing in Italy to prevent the infection from consumptive patients, were probably not enacted originally without a sufficient cause. We seem to be approaching to that state which first made such restrictions necessary, and in the further course of time, the disease will probably fall off again, both in virulency and frequency.

§ 31. The younger part of the female sex are liable to a disease very much resembling a true consumption, and from which it is difficult to distinguish it; but this disease is curable by steel and bitters. A criterion of true phthisis has been sought for in the state of the teeth; but the exceptions to that rule are numerous. An unusual dilatation of the pupil of the eye, is the most certain characteristic.

§ 32. Sydenham asserts, that the bark did not more certainly cure an intermittent, than riding did a consumption. We must not deny the truth of an assertion, from such authority, but we must conclude that the disease was more easily curable a century ago than it is at present.

§ 33. If the Digitalis is no longer useful in consumptive cases, it must be that I know not how to manage it, or that the disease is more fatal than formerly; for it would be hard to deny the testimony cited at page 9. I wish others would undertake the enquiry.

§ 34. When phthisis is accompanied with anasarca, or when there is reason to suspect hydrothorax, the Digitalis will often relieve the sufferings, and prolong the life of the patient.

§ 35. Many years ago, during an attendance upon Mr. B——, of a consumptive family, and himself in the last stage of a phthisis; after he was so ill as to be confined to his chamber, his breathing became so extremely difficult and distressing, that he wished rather to die than to live, and urged me warmly to devise some mode to relieve him. Suspecting serous effusion to be the cause of this symptom, and he being a man of sense and resolution, I fully explained my ideas to him, and told him what kind of operation might afford him a chance of relief; for I was then but little acquainted with the Digitalis. He was earnest for the operation to be tried, and with the assistance of Mr. Parrott, a very respectable surgeon of this place, I got an opening made between the ribs upon the lower and hinder part of the thorax. About a pint of fluid was immediately discharged, and his breath became easy. This fluid coagulated by heat.

After some days a copious purulent discharge issued from the opening, his cough became less troublesome, his expectoration less copious, his appetite and strength returned, he got abroad, and the wound, which became very troublesome, was allowed to heal.

He then undertook a journey to London; whilst there he became worse: returned home, and died consumptive some weeks afterwards.

PUERPERAL ANASARCA.

§ 36. This disease admits of an easy and certain cure by the Digitalis.

§ 37. This species of dropsy may originate from other causes than child birth. In the beginning of last March, a gentleman at Wolverhampton desired my advice for very large and painful swelled legs and thighs. He was a temperate man, not of a dropsical habit, had great pain in his groins, and attributed his complaints to a fall from his horse. He had taken diuretics, and the strongest drastic purgatives with very little benefit. Considering the anasarca as caused by the diseased inguinal glands, I ordered common poultice and mercurial ointment to the groins, three grains of pulv. fol. Digitalis night and morning, and a cooling diuretic decoction in the day-time. He soon lost his pain, and the swellings gradually subsided.

THE END.

FOOTNOTES:

See an original and valuable treatise by Dr. Fowler, entitled, Medical Reports of the Effects of Tobacco.

Many years ago I communicated to my friend, Dr. Percival, an account of some trials of breathing fixed air in consumptive cases. The results were published by him in the second Vol. of his very useful Essays Medical and Experimental, and have since been copied into other publications. I take this opportunity of acknowledging that I suspect myself to have been mistaken in the nature of the disease there mentioned to have been cured. I believe it was a case of Vomica, and not a true Phthisis that was cured. The Vomica is almost always curable. The fixed air corrects the smell of the matter, and very shortly removes the hectic fever. My patients not only inspire it, but I keep large jars of the effervescing mixture constantly at work in their chambers.

www.ingramcontent.com/pod-product-compliance
Lightning Source LLC
LaVergne TN
LVHW092047060526
838201LV00047B/1280